1776–1976

A Cartoon History of
United States Foreign Policy

1776–1976

A Cartoon History of United States Foreign Policy

BY THE EDITORS OF
THE FOREIGN POLICY
ASSOCIATION

With an Introduction by
Daniel P. Moynihan

WILLIAM MORROW AND COMPANY, INC.
New York

The Foreign Policy Association is a private, nonprofit, nonpartisan educational organization. For over half a century, the Association has worked to stimulate wider interest, greater understanding and more effective participation by American citizens in world affairs. FPA sponsors a wide variety of programs and publications analyzing the problems of American foreign policy. It works closely with many other public and private organizations and with the nation's schools and colleges in its educational effort. The Association strives to air different viewpoints impartially; it advocates none.

Daniel P. Moynihan is U.S. Ambassador to the United Nations.

Excerpts of Chapters 6 through 11 from the text of *A Cartoon History of United States Foreign Policy Since World War I,* by the Editors of the Foreign Policy Association, are reprinted by permission of Random House, Inc. Copyright © 1967 by Foreign Policy Association.

Printed in the United States of America.

3 4 5   79 78 77 76

Library of Congress Cataloging in Publication Data

Main entry under title:

A Cartoon history of United States foreign policy,
    1776-1976

    Bibliography: p.
    Includes index.

    1. United States—Foreign relations—Caricatures and cartoons.   2. American wit and humor, Pictorial.   I. Foreign Policy Association.
E183.9.C37   327.73   75-22458
ISBN 0-688-02976-0
ISBN 0-688-07976-8 pbk.

Acknowledgments

Many individuals, organizations and sources contributed to making this book possible, and it is a pleasure for the Foreign Policy Association to acknowledge their role.

The most valuable of the sources consulted and drawn upon were: Thomas A. Bailey's *A Diplomatic History of the American People;* Robert H. Ferrell's *American Diplomacy, A History*; William Murrell's *A History of American Graphic Humor*; *The History of the Nineteenth Century in Caricature* by Arthur Bartlett Maurice and F. T. Cooper; *A Century of Political Cartoons: Caricature in the United States from 1800 to 1900* by Allan Nevins and Frank Weitenkampf; and *The Ungentlemanly Art: A History of American Political Cartoons* by Stephen Hess and Milton Kaplan.

A number of organizations cooperated generously to make their cartoon resources available. These included: the American Antiquarian Society, Culver Pictures, The Granger Collection, the Houghton Library of Harvard University, the Historical Society of Pennsylvania, the Library Company of Philadelphia, the Library of Congress, The New-York Historical Society, The New York Public Library and Rothco Cartoons.

Among the individuals who made cartoons available or helped track them down, we are particularly indebted to the contemporary artists whose work is represented in this book and to the following persons: Mrs. Fred Ellis; Thomas Faye of the American Newspaper Guild; Alan Fern, Chief of the Prints Division, Library of Congress; Pat Finnegan of Scripps-Howard; Mrs. Carol W. Hazen of the Princeton University Library; John M. Henry of the Hoover Presidential Library Association, Inc.; Roberts Jackson of Culver Pictures; the staff of The New York Public Library: in particular, Miss Elizabeth E. Roth, Curator of the Prints Division, Miss Faye Simkin and John Miller; Miss Stefanie A. Munsing, Curator of Prints and

Drawings, Library Company of Philadelphia; and Ron Wolin, Executive Director of the Cartoonists Guild.

Separate mention is due Miss Gwen Crowe and Miss Ann Monjo, associate editors of the FPA staff, who successfully managed the complex and laborious task of obtaining cartoon permission rights.

Finally, and above all, we wish to acknowledge the signal and indispensable contribution of Miss Nancy L. Hoepli, senior editor of the FPA, who selected the cartoons that appear in this volume and wrote the text that accompanies them.

Contents

Contents

Introduction

At this remove in time it seems a bit hard to add further to the faults ascribed to William Marcy Tweed, but it does seem to be the case that he gave political cartoons the worst kind of good reputation. He did not worry, he told a lieutenant, about what the papers wrote about him. It was that cartoonist Thomas Nast. "My constituents," Tweed explained, "can't read."

Ever since—I shall be happy to be proved wrong in this—it has been assumed that cartoons had a relation to serious political comment rather like that of comic strips to the novel. The implications of the original Italian term, *cartone,* still linger: "a drawing on stout paper made as a design for a painting . . . to be executed in fresco or oil. . ." (OED) Not, that is, a finished work; not, certainly, of high seriousness. We may note that as the editorial page of the nation's most prominent newspaper aspired to ever Higher Seriousness, its cartoon disappeared. Yet so, some say, did many of its readers. Correspondingly, one of the brightest and surely most influential editorial pages in the nation today is that of *The Washington Post.* Just possibly this could be connected with the fact that the *Post* has also, in Herblock, one of the brightest and most influential editorial cartoonists in the nation.

Even so, cartooning continues to be regarded in the title of the indispensable study by Stephen Hess and Milton Kaplan as *The Ungentlemanly Art.* And not just in the United States, but also in Britain, from which the American tradition in political cartoons derives. Consider the entry in the Thirteenth Edition of the *Encyclopaedia Britannica* on James Gillray, whose influence is much to be seen in the early pages of this collection (and echoed in Yardley's splendid reenactment a century and one-half later). The ideas embodied in Gillray's work, the entry tells us, are "sublime and poetically magnificent in their intensity of meaning." His sketches, we learn, are "real works of art." A quality whereby he is "honourably distinguished in the history of caricature," which is to say, not like the others. Years later Max Beerbohm, in an "Epistle Dedicatory to Britannia" introducing his collection *A Survey*, observed with fine resignation:

> You say that you have always frowned on *some* of my drawings? True, Madam; and thank you for reminding me. Over some in every batch you have frowned, murmuring a fine and a favourite phrase of yours: "Not in the very best of taste."

Not indeed. As in life. It was not in the very best taste for President Johnson to display his operation scar for White House reporters that day in 1966, and it may not have been in the very best of taste for David Levine to seize on the incident. But the result may be the hardest and truest statement about the Vietnam war to emerge from that long travail.

There are many such statements in this absorbing *A Cartoon History of United States Foreign Policy 1776–1976*, which is no less a history for being irresistibly interesting. It is more than a political history, of course, for cartooning is an art, if not always a sublime one. Thus we see here the beginning of an American style as early as 1832, when James Akin, portraying the United States as Brother Jonathan confronting Wellington, the British prime minister, opts for psychological realism rather than extravagance. Brother Jonathan is a Maine fisherman or perhaps a salt-water farmer. Nothing grand, but no fool, and above all, no toady. An allegorical era ensues, and then, towards the end of the century, a kind of false realism, given to racial stereotypes and affecting a kind of insular arrogance we once discerned in the British. The influence of Darwinian ideas is to be seen, for example, in Grant Hamilton's 1898 depiction of Spain as a bloody and prognathous semi-beast. (This fate particularly befell the Irish during the nineteenth century, whose jaws jutted and jutted until the creature was indeed very apelike.) Darling and Fitzpatrick restore civility on this score but continue in the development of an American style which is at once realistic and fanciful, culminating (is that too presumptuous a term?) in the present profusion of talent—Oliphant, Rosen, Mauldin, Szep, Wright, Fischetti, to name only a few particular favorites—to be found in this teeming volume. Walt Kelly is here, too, for genius will not be stayed!

Here, then, is the work of America's greatest political cartoonists, and present throughout is that creation of their collective genius, Uncle Sam, the symbol of the American nation, the single undisputable contribution of political cartoonists to the political culture. Not quite in the best of taste. Benjamin Franklin would perhaps have approved, but even Jefferson, one feels, would have liked someone more, well, Ciceronian. Nor yet a gentleman: certainly not by the standards of the Sons of the Cincinnati. A merchant, rather. Avuncular rather than dignified; democratic rather than republican. The name, we can now agree, comes from "Uncle" Sam Wilson, a Troy merchant who sold and shipped supplies to the U.S.

government during the war of 1812. He so labeled his casks, and "U.S." became "Uncle Sam" after the local provisioner. Hess and Kaplan offer the judgment that Brother Jonathan was a precursor. At first a country bumpkin sort, adopted in defiance of the original derisive intent. The first known cartoon of Uncle Sam dates from 1832; the first in the present collection dates from 1846, although Akin in 1832 does refer to "Uncle." There was no turning back. The character becomes more, not less, common. He appears repeatedly in the last pages of this collection. Unless I am mistaken, it is he—and none other—clad in armor, Don Quixote-like, in the very last cartoon.

Allan Nevins thought Uncle Sam a disgrace, a "crude stereotype" that denies the complexity of the modern nation. And yet he hangs in there, undefeated, and essentially unchallenged—as much so in the press of Russia and China—and on the stage there as well—as in our own. Does some instinct tell us that, such as they are, these are our roots and had best not be forgot? Let each reader judge, and allow me to encourage the exercise. I am a New Yorker, raised in the city. I worked once for the governor in the state capitol in Albany, a few miles south and on the other side of the river from Troy. I like Uncle Sam, and connect with him. I know the farms where his beef came from; know what his warehouses were like (Troy hasn't changed that much); know what the Hudson river sloops were like that would have carried his cargo. But what about the citizens of Hawaii or Oregon, New Mexico or North Dakota? Any connection? If not, does a better representative come to mind?

This, of course, is not for us to say in the first instance. It is up to the cartoonist to offer alternatives; our opportunity for judgment comes thereafter. We shall see. In the meantime, my loyalties are unshaken. Uncle Sam may be crude, but he is no caricature. As I watch his progress through this volume, he seems to me an emphatic witness to the central subject of the cartoonist's art, which Beerbohm described simply as "politics and the deplorable part which human nature plays in politics. . . ."

DANIEL P. MOYNIHAN

West Davenport, New York
June, 1975

1776–1976

A Cartoon History of United States Foreign Policy

1

In the Beginning

America's greatest liquid assets are the oceans on either side of the continent. This has been true throughout much of our two-hundred-year history. But when the nation was founded, there was ocean on only one side and a vast virgin continent on the other. The western wilderness between the Alleghenies and the Mississippi was home to Indians and Frenchmen. Both constantly threatened the lives of American colonists. Unless they joined together for their defense and security, the good people of the eight colonies—New England, New York, New Jersey, Pennsylvania, Maryland, Virginia, North and South Carolina—had little chance of survival. This was the message carried by the first American political cartoon. It was reportedly drawn by Benjamin Franklin and appeared in his newspaper in 1754.

Franklin's "Snake Device" was soon reprinted in newspapers as far away as New York and Boston. In those days Boston, a bustling seaport with a population of twenty thousand, was a week's journey from Philadelphia.

Benjamin Franklin. *The Pennsylvania Gazette,* May 9, 1754.

During the Revolution, "Join, or Die" again became the rallying cry, and Franklin's slogan was frequently copied. This time around, the colonists were united against the British. And the hereditary foe of colonial days, the French, supplied the revolutionaries with much of the money and most of the gunpowder that kept their struggle alive.

When France declared war on Great Britain in 1793, America faced a choice: jump in and help France or aid Britain. It did neither. President Washington set the ship of state on a course away from Old World embroilments and issued a Proclamation of Neutrality.

The United States and Britain reestablished commercial relations in 1794. An outraged France retaliated by seizing American merchant ships and manhandling their crews. War seemed imminent. To avoid disaster, President John Adams in 1797 dispatched a three-man commission to France.

The trio was received in Paris by three mysterious men, "X," "Y," and "Z," accompanied by a beautiful woman. Apparently puppets of the French foreign minister, Talleyrand, the Frenchmen asked the Americans to pay a bribe to get negotiations started. The outraged Americans relayed the demand back to President Adams, who made it public.

Americans, infuriated by Talleyrand's insolence, called for war. The country's mood is reflected in this contemporary cartoon. It shows a five-headed monster, symbolizing France's five-man ruling Directory, demanding money of the firm, dignified Americans. At the right, a devil, a Negro, and a Jacobin are seated at a "civic feast," eating frogs. A terrible Goddess of Liberty guards the guillotine and one of its victims. In one hand she is holding the Tricolor and a liberty cap.

Cinque-tetes, or the Paris Monster

Anonymous, 1798.

For two and a half years America engaged in an undeclared war with France. The Francophile Jeffersonians came in for their share of abuse. The ruling Federalists called them "frog-eating, man-eating, blood-drinking cannibals," "Jacobins," and "Gallic jackals." In a Federalist cartoon, which probably appeared during the presidential campaign of 1800, Jefferson is shown kneeling before the "altar of Gallic despotism." A letter to Mazzei falls from his hand. (Jefferson wrote his Italian friend that the Federalist Administration was reactionary. To his embarrassment, the letter was intercepted and made public.) Jefferson is about to cast the Constitution into the flames. At the last minute an American eagle wrests the document from his hand.

The Providential Detection

Anonymous, 1800.

3

With Britain and France again at war in 1803, the United States found itself squarely in the middle. For a time the middle was a good place to be. American merchants enjoyed a boom. But within two years the belligerents' crossfire of blockades and counterblockades caught Americans amidships.

Most odious of all to Americans was the British policy of impressment. British warships regularly stopped American merchantmen and dragged off so-called British subjects. The British navy was chronically short of hands on its "floating hells." The pay was poor, the food wretched, the discipline brutal. All told, some eight thousand to ten thousand American citizens were seized. Many were killed in action or died of maltreatment.

The blame was not all Britain's. American shippers were also in need of manpower. They encouraged British sailors to desert by offering them bounties, higher wages, and better working conditions.

The impressment-desertion controversy came to a head in 1807, when the British fired upon the American frigate *Chesapeake* and seized four men—three of whom were Americans.

A wave of indignation swept America. Jefferson ordered all British warships out of American waters. He demanded reparations and the total abandonment of impressment. The last demand was too much for the British. They accused the United States of meddling in domestic policy and flatly refused. Since continued submission to British abuses was unthinkable and war equally unthinkable, Jefferson chose a compromise course—economic coercion.

In December, 1807, Congress passed an Embargo Act. The act virtually prohibited the export of any goods from the United States by land or sea. Federalist New England was unalterably opposed to the embargo. Trade was its bread and butter. Instead of protecting the lifeline, the embargo severed it. Thousands of sailors lost their jobs, shipyards closed, soup kitchens were set up, bankruptcies and suicides were commonplace.

A commentary on those parlous times appeared in *Hugginiana,* which was published in 1808. The author, a barber and wigmaker by the name of John Richard Desborus Huggins, felt equally at home with pen as with razor. He wrote many witty and impudent advertisements which appeared in New York newspapers. He also commissioned and sold cartoons at his shop. The cartoon below, by one of the best draftsmen of his day, Elkanah Tisdale, who was employed by Huggins, ridicules Jefferson and his embargo. It shows Thomas 1st leaping out of the barber's chair, apparently enraged by the Ship News. Huggins (Desborus 1st) is trying to give Jefferson a shave. In the background is a would-be President getting his hair queued by Prince Paris-eney. Waiting their turns are Napoleon Duane and the late captain of the ship *Hare.* Next to them stands a wig block supporting the Imperial crown. Hanging from the ceiling are toads and prairie dogs.

4

"D--n, d--n, the Author & Publisher I say!"

Elkanah Tisdale, 1807.

The embargo hurt Britain as well as New England. Textile mills were forced to close. And British colonies were cut off from their American suppliers.

Napoleon was delighted. What was bad for Britain was good for France. The French emperor even pretended to help the United States enforce its embargo. He seized American ships in French harbors on the pretext that they were undoubtedly British craft in disguise. Within a year, 1808–1809, he had confiscated American vessels and cargoes worth $10 million.

Most Americans considered the embargo a failure. New Englanders were the most outspoken against it, although they in fact made considerable profit from illicit trade. The embargo, they charged, was reducing the country to rags . . .

Non Intercourse or Dignified Retirement

"Peter Pencil," 1809.

And it was enriching the two countries it was supposed to harm . . .

Intercourse or Impartial Dealings

"Peter Pencil," 1809.

At the end of Jefferson's term, Congress repealed the embargo. Objectionable as it was, the embargo did relieve impressment and helped postpone war, if only temporarily. And it contributed to Britain's subsequent repeal of the odious Orders in Council. The orders had given British ships carte blanche to detain neutral American ships and confiscate any cargo going to or coming from France or its colonies.

When Madison assumed the Presidency in 1809, the War Hawks in the West were clamoring for action. Though least affected by impressment, they were most outraged by the practice. The South and Southwest joined them in urging the President to break relations with England. Only Federalist New England deplored the war talk and opposed Madison's tilt toward France.

The passage of a ninety-day embargo on trade with England in April, 1812, further embittered New England. Whatever way the letters of *embargo* (known as the terrapin policy) were twisted—"o-grab-me" or "go-bar-em"—in New England they spelled "mob-rage."

OGRABME, or, The American Snapping-turtle

"A" (Alexander Anderson), 1813.

Two days after Britain repealed the Orders in Council but before the news reached Washington, the United States declared war on Britain.

Federalist New England denounced "Mr. Madison's war." It kept the militia at home and even sold provisions to the British. The Madisonians, meantime, exulted in every Napoleonic victory. By pinning the British down, the French aided America's "second war for independence" and opened the path for our invasion of Canada.

The invasion of Canada backfired disastrously. The British and Canadians hurled the American armies back from the frontier. By 1814 the United States was desperately defending its own territory.

At sea, America did somewhat better. Late in 1813 an American fleet commanded by Oliver Hazard Perry met a British force on Lake Erie. "We have met the enemy and they are ours," Perry reported to General Harrison. Overnight Perry (whose name was the same as that of a popular beverage made from pear juice) was a national hero. His victory gave the United States control of Lake Erie . . .

Brother Jonathan Administering a Salutary Cordial to John Bull

Amos Doolittle (Yankee-Doodle Scratcher), 1813.

. . . And it was a source of momentary discomfort to King George III, who is shown in the cartoon below seated on a commode. The king's wife, for whom one of the sunken warships was named, is spraying him with Perry. The sprays are labeled with the names of American ships.

Queen Charlotte and Johnny Bull Got their dose of Perry

William Charles, 1813.

In single-ship duels with the British, the swift American sloops and oversized frigates also scored. The British had to send in fresh reinforcements.

John Bull making a new Batch of Ships to send to the Lakes

William Charles, 1814.

Peace discussions had begun shortly after the first gun was fired. But in over two years the negotiators made little headway. In October, 1814, they received news in Ghent, where they were meeting, that the British army was headed for Washington. The Redcoats had conquered Alexandria where they replenished their stores.

Johnny Bull and the Alexandrians

William Charles, 1814.

On hearing the news that Washington had fallen, the British hardened their peace terms. These included exclusive control of the Great Lakes and a huge Indian buffer zone in the North. Even New England was outraged by the arrogant British demands.

The American victory on Lake Champlain forced the British to back down. Although they still had the upper hand, the British wanted out. Both sides were exhausted. And on Christmas Eve, 1814, the Treaty of Ghent was signed. The pact more or less restored the status quo ante bellum. There was no mention of either neutral rights or impressment.

Before news of the peace reached the United States (the first permanent transatlantic cable would not be laid for another fifty years), Andrew Jackson won a smashing victory over superior British forces at New Orleans on January 8, 1815.

John Bull Before New Orleans

William Charles, 1815.
(An American rifleman and a French ally haul a wigless John Bull out of the bog.)

Some Americans erroneously believed the United States had whipped the British into submission and won the war.

New England, on learning it had to give up neither territory nor fishing rights, hailed the standoff truce with unrestrained joy. Moreover, the hated embargo had been repealed. That event prompted John Wesley Jarvis, a well-known portrait painter of the day, to design the first cartoon prepared specifically for newspaper reproduction in America. Until commercial lithography—a simple and cheap reproduction process—was introduced in 1822, artists engraved, etched, or cut their drawings on steel, copper, and wood. It was a slow, laborious process. The artist or engraver sold the cartoons by mail or in retail stores. Lithograph cartoons made their first appearance in 1828 and were very popular for fifty years. They were published on separate sheets and sold for twelve and a half to twenty-five cents apiece.

Jarvis's cartoon shows a terrapin (symbol of the embargo) floating on its back and clutching the body of Madison. The President managed to sever the turtle's head but in the process lost an ear.

The Death of the Embargo

" TO THE GRAVE GO SHAM PROTECTORS OF " FREE TRADE AND SAILORS' RIGHTS"—AND ALL THE PEOPLE SAY AMEN !"

John Wesley Jarvis, 1814.

The cartoon, which ran in the *New York Evening Post,* was accompanied by a verse by a Federal satirist:

> Down to the grave t' atone for sin
> Jemmy must go with Terrapin,
> Bear *him* but off, and we shall see
> *Commerce restor'd, and Sailors Free!*

"Jemmy" Madison remained afloat for another three years. In 1817 he was succeeded by James Monroe.

2

"Ho for the Halls of the Montezumas"

President Monroe ushered in the "Era of Good Feeling" in 1817. For a dozen years there was little to entice the satirist's pen or the cartoonist's pencil. The United States' acquisition of the Floridas and of Spain's vague claims to the disputed Oregon territory in 1819 created barely a ripple. Nor was there excessive protest over America's surrender, in return, of its shadowy claim to Texas.

In Europe, with Napoleon out of the way, the long-exiled monarchs of Russia, Austria, Prussia, Sweden, France, and Spain were back on their thrones. Several banded together with England in a Holy Alliance and promptly stamped out former liberties. The United States was not unduly worried until France suppressed a revolution in Spain in 1823. That gave the United States a bad case of war jitters, for rumor had it that a Franco-Spanish army was preparing to descend on the Americas to crush the infant Latin American republics.

The rumor prompted Monroe to issue a warning to Europe, the genesis of the famous Monroe Doctrine. The American continents were "henceforth not to be considered as subjects for future colonization by any European powers," Monroe declared in the course of an annual message to Congress in 1823. This was the first clear American foreign policy statement of global proportions. And for twenty years it was largely ignored.

Monroe might not have risked defying Europe if he had not been certain of the British navy's support. Britain was carrying on a lucrative trade with the new Spanish-American markets. And London was just as anxious as Washington to prevent France or any other European power from interfering.

The rumor of a Franco-Spanish invasion proved ill-founded, and the American foreign-relations front remained calm throughout most of the '30s. It was a period of breakneck internal expansion. Britain's prime minister, the Duke of Wellington, occasionally blustered about British

15

rights to timber and land in the disputed northern portion of Maine. But Brother Jonathan (a descendant of the revolutionary Yankee Doodle and nephew of Uncle Sam) did not seem overly concerned.

A general arguing of the Maine question, or John Bull's Bully trying to frighten Jonathan out of Title & Timber

James Akin, 1832.

One piece of unfinished business with France was cleared up in 1831. For years Washington had been trying to collect compensation for the American ships seized by Napoleon. A claim of 25 million francs payable in six installments was finally agreed upon. But France welched on the first payment. An irate President Andrew Jackson threatened to "seize" French property.

Jackson, the Hero of New Orleans, who became the country's seventh President in 1829, had a powerful following in the West among frontier farmers, backwoodsmen, plain folk. To the small man he was a forceful democratic leader. To his detractors he was hotheaded, high-handed, capricious, and dictatorial.

Jackson's allegedly dictatorial ways got him in trouble with the Senate. In a dispute over the Bank of the United States, Jackson claimed that as President he was the "official representative of the American people." That was too much for the Senate, and at the urging of Henry Clay it censured the President for an unconstitutional assertion of Executive power.

Symptoms of a Locked Jaw

D. C. J[ohnston], c. 1834.

17

Jackson's handling of the French claim, by contrast, was widely supported. When France demanded that Jackson apologize for threatening France, the country applauded "Old Hickory's" two-fisted reaction.

A "Hickory" Apology

James Akin, 1836.

Thanks to the friendly mediation of the British in 1836, a confrontation with Louis Philippe's government was avoided.

The Old Lion and the Cock what won't fight

Anonymous, 1836.

The 1840s ushered in the era of Manifest Destiny. "The great American disease," some called it. Others termed it a lay religion or an imperialistic crusade. Despite prior claims by France, Spain, Russia, Great Britain, and Mexico, most Americans believed deep down that the entire continent was destined to be theirs.

Manifest Destiny was a major issue in the presidential campaign of 1844. The future of several disputed territories was debated. These included a segment of the Oregon territory. Oregon, which stretched from the 49th parallel as far north as the 54° 40′ line, was under joint American-British occupation. Between 1840 and 1845 the number of American traders, trappers, and settlers in the area had increased tenfold, from five hundred to five thousand.

America's relations with independent Texas were also in flux. In 1821 Mexico had made the mistake of giving Moses Austin a grant of land on which to settle three hundred families. Fourteen years later there were thirty thousand white settlers in Texas. When the Mexican dictator Santa Anna tried to establish a strong, centralized government in Mexico in 1835, the Texans revolted and declared their independence. They received some unneutral help from America.

President Jackson recognized the independence of the Lone Star, but he hesitated to take up Texas' offer to be annexed.

Nine years later, in 1845, Congress and President Tyler accepted the offer. The Lone Star was invited to merge with "the constellation of the stars and stripes."

The signing, which took place three days before the end of President Tyler's term, did nothing to improve Mexican-American relations. Tyler's successor, President Polk, sent his representative to Mexico to negotiate. There was the matter of Mexico's unpaid claims, the future of California, and the Texas boundary. Mexico rebuffed the President's envoy. Thereupon Polk ordered General Zachary Taylor to march right into the area of Texas claimed by Mexico as far as the Rio Grande. As the troops advanced, enthusiastic crowds shouted "Mexico or Death!" and "Ho for the Halls of the Montezumas."

Uncle Sam's Taylorifics

Edward Williams Clay, 1846.

General Taylor made camp near the mouth of the Rio Grande, opposite the Mexican town of Matamoras. He was eyeball to eyeball with the Mexican commander, General Santa Anna.

20

The Mexican Commander enjoying the Prospect opposite Matamoras

G. Thomas, 1846.

Following a skirmish between the opposing forces, the United States declared war in May, 1846. California and New Mexico fell easily from Mexico's feeble grasp. Elsewhere the going was tougher. In September, 1847, American troops led by General Winfield Scott captured Mexico City. But peace was still several months away.

Under the terms of the Treaty of Guadalupe Hidalgo, Mexico ceded New Mexico and California outright and recognized the Rio Grande as the new boundary of Texas.

Despite the annexationist fever rampant in the country, some observers, among them the humorous weekly *Yankee Doodle*, felt a twinge of sympathy for the Mexicans.

Plucked

THE MEXICAN EAGLE BEFORE THE WAR!   THE MEXICAN EAGLE AFTER THE WAR!

Anonymous. *Yankee Doodle*, 1847.

The peace treaty had no sooner been signed than gold was discovered in California. Americans weren't the only ones bitten by the gold bug. A few thousand Europeans joined the rush.

Defence of the California Bank

Anonymous, 1849.

This contemporary cartoon shows San Francisco Bay being invaded by foreigners, represented by the European heads of state. Queen Victoria is shown arriving by bull, singing a ditty to the tune of "Oh Susanna!" She is followed by a Russian bear with the head of Czar Nicholas. Flying above her is a bird with the head of Louis Napoleon, and Isabella II of Spain is swimming toward the shore. A huge rattlesnake with the head of President Taylor warns them off.

A water route to the West was a major preoccupation in Washington at that time. The country urgently needed access by sea to the vast new American territory on the Pacific. The logical place for a man-made canal linking the two oceans was the Isthmus of Panama.

Central America and the Caribbean were highly volatile areas in those days. A spate of revolutions had weakened Europe's hold on its colonies. Haiti, once part of the French empire, had exchanged one tyranny for another. The mushroom empire of Soulouque, last of Haiti's Negro emperors, whose court was a caricature of Napoleon's, was the object of ridicule in America. The cartoon below is a study in contemporary stereotypes.

Soloque, Emperor of Hayti, creating a Grand Duke

Anonymous, c. 1856.

The biggest treasure in the Caribbean was Cuba. Together with Puerto Rico, it was the sole remnant of the once great Spanish American empire. "The Pearl of the Antilles" was awash with sugar and molasses. And it commanded the crossroads of the trade routes through the Caribbean. It could one day control traffic through the isthmus.

Before the war with Mexico, America had been defensive and protective toward Cuba. After the war, "The World's Sugar Bowl" attracted the sticky fingers of the sons of Manifest Destiny. The South, in particular, had an eye on the island as a logical spot for spreading slavery.

President Pierce, a Democrat, joined in the expansionist furor and was all for annexing Cuba. But political considerations intervened. Pierce had already rammed the Kansas-Nebraska bill through Congress over the outraged protests of the North. The bill opened a vast territory to the possibility of slavery. A second sellout to the slavery interests would be politically suicidal.

It was during Pierce's Administration that the country's three top diplomats in Europe sent the State Department a confidential report on Cuba, recommending that it be wrested from Spain. The contents of the dispatch were leaked and became known as the Ostend Manifesto (although it was signed at Aix-la-Chapelle).

James Buchanan, who was Minister to Britain at the time, was one of the drafters of the manifesto. This endeared him to the conservative Southern Democrats and helped catapult him into the country's highest office. The former Federalist was elected on the Democratic ticket, and in 1857 he became the only bachelor and only Pennsylvanian to make it to the Presidency.

In three of his four annual messages to Congress, President Buchanan called for the purchase of Cuba. But it was not to be. The Dred Scott decision in 1857 intensified the slavery debate in the country. The Republicans in Congress would probably not have agreed to accept Cuba even as a gift. The Southern Democrats were equally adamant about the importance of acquiring Cuba at almost any price. Neither side would compromise. As the country lurched toward civil war, the issue of Cuba was gradually eclipsed.

A Serviceable Garment, or Reverie of a Bachelor

Louis Maurer, 1856.

3

The Uncivil War and Its Aftermath

At four-thirty on the morning of April 12, 1861, the South Carolinians fired on Fort Sumter. The Civil War had begun. Britain became the focus of American diplomacy. Which way would Britain go? The answer was critical to both sides. The Confederacy pressed London to intervene. Lincoln's fervent hope was that London would remain neutral.

John Bull Makes A Discovery

Currier & Ives, c. 1861.

The British upper classes and the majority of English journals were unabashedly pro-South. As they saw the war, the South was the underdog with the more appealing cause, namely self-determination for a minority. And there were sound economic reasons for supporting the South. Eighty percent of the cotton used by the British textile industry came from the southern states. Moreover, Britain could undoubtedly get more favorable terms of trade from the Confederacy than it could from the North. Washington's passage of the moderately protective Morrill Tariff in 1861 had infuriated the British. As Britain's Prime Minister Palmerston summed it up: "We do not like slavery, but we want cotton, and we dislike very much your Morrill tariff."

A week after the attack on Fort Sumter, Lincoln threw up a blockade of the seven secessionist states. London and the other maritime powers recognized the blockade and in so doing dealt a heavy blow to the Confederate cause. Shortly thereafter the British issued a proclamation of neutrality.

The rout at Bull Run was only the first of a series of defeats for the demoralized Union forces. So when the news of the *Trent* affair reached the North, there was joyful hysteria. Captain Charles Wilkes, commander of the USS *San Jacinto,* acting wholly on his own, had intercepted the British mail steamer *Trent* and kidnapped two of the South's ablest statesmen, Mason and Slidell.

The cartoon above is from the November 30, 1861, issue of *Harper's Weekly,* one of a number of weekly magazines which made their appearance in America in the 1850s and '60s. By 1865 the weeklies had driven lithograph prints almost out of existence. Illustrated daily journalism remained a rarity until 1872, and it was only in the campaign of 1884 that the newspaper cartoon became a major force, according to William Murrell, author of *A History of American Graphic Humor.*

Wilkes's caper was a bold stroke but one that almost led to war with Britain. London demanded an apology for the affront to the Union Jack. International law appeared to be on Britain's side. After an agonized debate, Lincoln's Cabinet decided to release the prisoners. A major diplomatic crisis of the war had ended.

In the fall of 1862, when the war was going badly for the North, England debated intervening and recognizing the Confederacy. But the Union victory over General Lee at Antietam persuaded the British to hold off.

France also contemplated intervention on behalf of the South. Napoleon III set up a puppet empire in Mexico in 1863. Its chances of survival would improve markedly if America were permanently divided. Napoleon tried to sell England on intervention, but by then London had cooled to the idea.

POLICEMAN WILKES, noticing by the last Number of *Harper's Weekly*, that the well-known Rogues, MASON and SLIDELL, were about to Pawn some of their late Employer's Property at Messrs. *Bull, Crapaud & Co.'s* Shop, kept a bright look-out for'ard, and nabbed them in the nick of time."

Harper's Weekly, 1861

He also approached Russia and was again turned down. Undaunted, Napoleon next turned to Washington and offered to mediate. Congress overwhelmingly rejected his offer and warned that any further meddling would be considered an unfriendly act.

The meddling on the part of France and Britain did not stop at the water's edge. It extended to the high seas. Confederate commerce destroyers, built in British shipyards and manned by British crews, were inflicting heavy casualties on Yankee traders. Britain had a law against the sale of battleships to belligerents. But the shipbuilders got around the law by not arming the ships until after they left Britain. The *Alabama,* one of the most famous of the raiders, alone burned, sank, or put out of commission over sixty Yankee ships.

The same Liverpool shipyard which built the *Alabama* was commissioned by the Confederacy to build ironclad steam warships equipped with powerful wrought-iron "piercers," or rams. Had the British government not intervened at the eleventh hour and detained the rams, the Confederacy might have broken the North's blockade and won its independence.

In contrast to the British government, which maintained at least a semblance of neutrality, Napoleon III secretly connived with the Confederates to supply warships. However, only one French ram reached Confederate hands—and that one too late to do much damage.

The North bitterly resented what it considered British and French breaches of neutrality. The resentment extended to Canada. Confederate agents in plainclothes used Canada as a base for raids across the border. American sentiment is reflected in this cartoon, which, like most cartoons of the '60s, made heavy use of allegory. The American eagle is perched on the rock of Liberty, surrounded by a Gallic cock, a monkey resembling Napoleon III, an angry British lion, and a Canadian unicorn.

Our Foreign Relations

Anthony Hochstein, 1864.

29

Napoleon had taken advantage of America's preoccupation with the Civil War to invade Mexico, overthrow the republican government, and install the Austrian puppet prince, Maximilian. Americans paid little attention at the time to France's defiance of the Monroe Doctrine; but when the Civil War ended, General Grant, among others, threatened to march down to Mexico and toss Maximilian out. Secretary of State Seward restrained the generals. But at the same time he applied pressure on Napoleon to make a prompt retreat.

Reconstruction—the old Map mended. Our soldier boys make a blanket of it and toss up Max and his Master.

William Newman. *Frank Leslie's Budget of Fun*, 1865.

Napoleon's Mexican adventure ended in 1867 with the withdrawal of the French troops and the execution of Maximilian by President Juarez's followers.

War with France was avoided. And the Republican Secretary of State had vindicated the Monroe Doctrine.

Seward was an expansionist. As soon as the guns were silent, he cast about for bases in the Caribbean. But Congress was not in an expansionist mood. It turned down opportunities to buy the Virgin Islands from Denmark, establish a protectorate over Haiti, and negotiate for a naval base with the Dominican Republic. Spain had reannexed the Dominican Republic in 1861 but withdrew voluntarily in 1865.

Seward's one great real-estate killing was the purchase of Alaska from Russia. "Seward's Icebox" was one of the nicer things Americans called the new territory. Why would anyone pay $7.2 million for "walrus-covered icebergs" in "a barren, worthless, God-forsaken region"? people asked. A contemporary cartoon shows Secretary Seward and President Johnson welcoming "representatives" of the new Alaska territory to Washington.

Our New Senators

SECRETARY SEWARD.—" My dear Mr. Kamskatea, you really must dine with me. I have some of the very finest tallow candles and the loveliest train oil you ever tasted, and my whale's blubber is exquisite—and pray bring your friend Mr. Seal along with you. The President will be one of the party."

Anonymous, 1867.

31

Seward defended the transaction and put on a convincing public education campaign. As Americans' knowledge of Alaska grew, so did their enthusiasm. When the time came to tally Congress's votes, Seward had more than he needed. It was America's last purchase of continental territory. And it was the first time the country acquired land without promising eventual incorporation into the Union. Historians called the Alaska Purchase the first portent of the imperialist expansion of the '90s.

When General Grant stepped into the Presidency in 1869, American relations with Britain could not have been worse. It was largely thanks to the careful diplomatic footwork of Secretary of State Hamilton Fish that a complete break was avoided.

At the top of the list of American grievances were the unsettled *Alabama* claims. Some Americans insisted on nothing less than all of Canada in *partial* settlement of those claims.

The deadlock in Anglo-American relations was broken in Washington in 1871 with the signing of a treaty. Britain formally expressed regret over the *Alabama* affair, and the claims were referred to an international tribunal.

In the first really great international arbitration of modern times, representatives of the United States, Britain, Switzerland, Brazil, and Italy met in Geneva. In September, 1872, the tribunal awarded the United States the sum of $15.5 million. The British were apoplectic.

The Apple of Discord at the Geneva Tribunal

Thomas Nast. *Harper's Weekly*, 1872.

The Treaty of Washington called for three other arbitrations. By the time the last award was announced, Anglo-American relations were back on an even keel.

For the next two decades Americans resumed their traditional policy of avoiding foreign entanglements. They were absorbed in their own affairs—taming half a continent, fighting Indians, building railroads, and putting up factories. So indifferent were most Americans to diplomacy in the '70s and '80s, historian Thomas Bailey notes, that the *New York Sun* in 1889 declared: "...The diplomatic service has outgrown its usefulness.... It is a costly humbug and sham." And the *New York Herald* in 1892 called on Washington to "Abolish our foreign Ministers! Recall our farcical diplomats."

The indifference to the outside world was reflected in the sadly neglected state of the U. S. Navy. What was left of the Civil War fleet was allowed to sit and rot.

Shipwrecked Patriotism

"G." *Puck,* 1882.

It was not until 1883 that the Congress broke down and appropriated funds for four modern steel ships.

The Navy had not been neglected for lack of dollars. Thanks to American customs duties, the nation's revenues far exceeded its expenses. Indeed, in 1887 the big problem facing Congress was what to do with the country's huge surplus.

The Opening of the Congressional Session

Tariff Monster.—Here I am again! What are you going to do with me?

Joseph Keppler. *Puck,* 1887.

The two political parties had different solutions. In the presidential campaign of 1888, in which trade was the major issue, Democrat Cleveland came out for lower tariffs. Republican Harrison was a high-tariff man. According to the Republicans, high tariffs meant high wages. If the "free trade" Democrats had their way, they warned, the country would soon be beset by rising unemployment and depression.

The Goose That Lays The Golden Eggs

Democratic Politician *(to Workingman)*—"Kill the Goose
and get all your Eggs at once."

Bernard Gillam, *Judge*, 1888.

The Republicans went so far as to accuse the Democrats of putting British interests above those of their own country. Britain was the leading free-trade nation at the time.

Cleveland and the Democrats countered that they were advocating not free trade but lower tariffs. They charged that high protective tariffs enriched the British at the expense of the American consumer. The American public was paying far more than necessary for goods which were imported in British bottoms. It was high time to break Britain's hold on the world's commerce.

At Last!

Joseph Keppler. *Puck*, 1888.

The charges and countercharges ignited a blaze of Anglophobia. Republicans warned Americans that a vote for Cleveland was a vote for England. Such accusations did not help Anglo-American relations. But the country was so consumed with domestic politics that it took little note of England's indignation. For several months the office of British ambassador to Washington was vacant.

By 1890 the era of postwar reconstruction was nearing its end. The last desirable free land was disappearing. And the curtain was about to rise on a new chapter in our nation's history.

4

Remember the **Maine***?*

Having subdued a continent, America's tremendous energy and expansive drive sought new outlets. Americans had a growing sense of national consciousness and of power. Didn't Darwin say, in effect, that the world belonged to the strongest and fittest? To be a world power, the country needed a navy, and the navy, to be effective, required bases. Washington began to look for targets of opportunity.

American imperialism had a number of previews before the main event. In 1889 the United States joined Britain and Germany in establishing a protectorate over Samoa. Four years later, Americans backed a rebellion against Hawaii's Queen Liliuokalani. Only one day after the uprising the American minister hoisted the Stars and Stripes over Honolulu. The outgoing Republican President Benjamin Harrison hastily sent a treaty of annexation to the Senate. But before the Senate could act, Harrison's successor, Grover Cleveland, who was an archfoe of imperialism, withdrew it.

Cleveland managed to keep the imperialists on a short leash. But by the end of his term in 1897 America was again feeling its muscle and raring to go. The country had recovered from the financial Panic of '93, and prosperity was going to its head. The new generation of Americans, moreover, was unscarred by war. The country had not fought a war since 1865; it had not fought a foreign war since the war with Mexico in 1848.

The United States did not have to look very hard or far to satisfy its expansionist appetite. The Cubans had been restive under Spanish misrule and had mounted a full-scale revolt in 1895. The Filipinos were also unhappy under Spanish rule, and they, too, had rebelled.

She Is Getting Too Feeble to Hold Them

J. S. Pughe. *Puck,* 1896.

Spain dispatched "Butcher" Weyler to Cuba to put down the rebellion. He promptly herded the population, including women and children, into barbed-wire reconcentration camps, where tens of thousands died.

Sensational exposés of Spanish brutality appeared in the yellow journals of Hearst and Pulitzer. The public clamored for war, and drowned out the voices of U. S. business and commercial interests who opposed it.

McKinley hoped to avoid a conflict by applying a bit of quiet diplomacy. His chances of succeeding were all but torpedoed when the U. S. battleship *Maine* blew up and sank in Havana harbor with over 250 officers and men aboard. (The cause of the explosion remains a mystery to this day, although it was widely assumed at the time to have been a Spanish mine.)

Passions in the country ran high. "Remember the *Maine!* To hell with Spain!" was the slogan of the hour. As some congressmen debated war, others gathered in the lobbies of the Capitol, according to historian Bailey, and sang "The Battle Hymn of the Republic" and "Hang General Weyler to a Sour Apple Tree as We Go Marching On." Pro-interventionists argued that the United States had a humanitarian duty to save Cubans from their Spanish oppressors. Opponents pointed out that we were in no position to lecture Spain on her treatment of Cubans, considering our own treatment of Indians.

Consistency

Joseph Keppler. *Puck*, 1891.

The Continental European powers were almost unanimous in disapproving the United States' aggressive stance. But they didn't want to offend Britain, or, for that matter, the United States. Outside of a fainthearted remonstrance to Washington and a plea for peace, they did little to help Spain. The Spanish premier, Sagasta, was on his own.

"The Boy Stood on the Burning Deck."

Charles Nelan. *The Herald* (New York), 1898.

Spain did bow to two U. S. demands—a temporary armistice and the lifting of the reconcentration order—but the hour was late. The public and political pressures on McKinley were enormous. Two days *after* receiving word of Spain's capitulation, on April 11, 1898, the President sent a war message to Congress. He underscored the urgent need to abate a nuisance at our door, to protect American trade and property in Cuba, and to eliminate a menace to our peace.

On April 19 Congress passed a joint resolution demanding Spain's withdrawal from Cuba. It recognized the island's freedom and disclaimed any intention to annex.

Make Him Walk Spanish
Uncle Sam—Now Git—Durn Ye!

Charles L. Bartholomew (Bart). *Minneapolis Journal,* 1898.

Whatever small hope Spain still harbored of salvaging its empire or at least its prestige was soon extinguished. Less than two weeks after Congress's joint declaration, Admiral Dewey sent the Spanish navy to the bottom of Manila Bay. The first blow for Cuban independence was struck on the other side of the globe.

After Dewey's incredible victory, the name of the game was no longer liberating Cuba but acquiring an empire. Many Americans liked the idea. They considered it America's Duty and Destiny to rescue the Spanish colonies.

The Spanish Brute Adds Mutilation to Murder

Grant Hamilton. *Judge*, 1898.

Other Americans saw no virtues in the United States' acquiring a burdensome family of dependents. McKinley himself had been unenthusiastic about going to war. Now he was undecided about how to handle his victory. He could return the Philippine Islands to Spanish misrule, annex them, or recognize their independence. The President waited for public sentiment to crystallize.

The Cares of a Growing Family

J. Campbell Cory. *The Bee*, 1898.

After prayerful consideration, McKinley concluded "that there was nothing left for us to do but to take them all, and to educate the Filipinos, and uplift and civilize and Christianize them . . ."

The foes of overseas expansion favored independence for the Philippines. They tried to convince themselves that American imperialism was a passing phase.

Our Expansive Uncle, But It's Only Temporary

William H. Walker. *Life,* 1899.

The anti-expansionists were a minority. Most Americans appeared to agree with Senator Lodge that "where the flag once goes up it must never come down." By the end of the century the United States had not only driven Spain out of Cuba; it had swallowed up Hawaii, the Philippines, Puerto Rico, Guam, Wake Island, and a chunk of Samoa. If there had ever been any doubt, by 1900 America was indisputably a Great Power.

5

From the Big Stick to the "War to End War"

A vast potential market beckoned in the Far East. Now that the United States was a Pacific power, it was in a position to claim a piece of the action. Pago Pago in Samoa provided a way station for U. S. trade with the South Pacific—New Zealand and Australia. Hawaii was a bridge between the West Coast and the Philippines. The Philippines gave America a window on eastern Asia.

The European imperialists had begun carving up the Chinese empire in earnest after China's poor showing in the Sino-Japanese War of 1894–1895. Britain was alarmed: it had by far the largest foreign-trade stake in the Far East. If nothing were done to stop the Europeans from acquiring long-term leaseholds in China and surrounding them with high tariff walls, Britain's trade would one day be strangulated. London reminded Washington of British support during the Spanish-American War, and suggested that Washington could reciprocate by supporting British efforts to keep China's ports open.

The United States twice refused, invoking its traditional policy of nonentanglement. But American merchants and missionaries were just as anxious as the British to have the United States intervene. They kept up the pressure on the State Department until the Secretary of State agreed to reconsider.

In a dramatic reversal of policy, Secretary John Hay in September, 1899, sent Open Door notes to the six powers with interests in China. He urged each one not to interfere with the commercial interests of the others in its particular sphere of influence. In a corollary to the first notes, delivered in 1900, Hay put the United States on record as supporting the territorial integrity of all China and commercial equality in all parts of the Chinese empire. In effect, Washington was trying to protect its own as well as Britain's access to the lucrative China trade. And it was attempting to forestall the dismemberment of China.

43

The danger of dismemberment was aggravated by the outbreak of the Boxer Rebellion in 1900. The Boxers were a group of fanatical Chinese who were out to kill the "foreign devils." The Czar took advantage of the ensuing chaos to dispatch his troops to Manchuria, allegedly to protect Russian lives and a segment of the all-but-completed Trans-Siberian Railroad.

Russia promised to withdraw its troops when the rebellion ended, but they were still there four years later. If Russia succeeded in occupying Manchuria, this would leave Japan dangerously exposed. In February, 1904, Tokyo mounted a damaging sneak attack on the Czarist fleet at Port Arthur, Manchuria. Two days later Japan declared war on Russia. The United States officially took a "wait and see" attitude.

A Story of the China Shop
An Artist's View of the Complications in the Far East

Uncle Sam, "Seems ter be a little trouble at the store to-day, boys."

Uncle Sam (to France, Germany, and England). " There he goes inside, boys; guess we'd better stay out fer a while."

Uncle Sam (to China). " Be careful you don't get mixed up in it."

China, " Hellup!"
Uncle Sam. " Jinkys! they're pulled him inside too. Don't git too near, boys."

5. Uncle Sam. "Never mind, boys. Don't go any nearer. We'll just wait a few days."

6. The Kaiser, et al. "Dot looks to usses like ve vait. Uncle Sammy was right, yes?"

Albert Levering. *Harper's Weekly,* 1904.

The United States had traditionally been friendly with both countries. But American sympathies were with the apparent underdogs, the Japanese. Washington suspected that the Russians intended to slam the Open Door in Manchuria, and a Japanese victory would spike that plan. President Roosevelt warned France and Germany to keep hands off. Britain didn't need a warning: it was allied with Japan.

The land war between Russia and Japan was fought on Chinese soil without a second thought to China's neutrality. Within months the Japanese had routed the Russians. But it cost them over 100,000 lives. Japan secretly asked President Roosevelt to mediate. The Russians were also anxious to end the carnage. And in the summer of 1905 Roosevelt met with representatives of the two sides in Portsmouth, New Hampshire.

The Peace of Portsmouth was a personal triumph for Roosevelt, although it strained U. S.-Japanese relations and won few friends in Russia.

The fact that both countries had turned to the United States underscored America's new role as a Pacific power. With vast interests to protect, the country's need for a water link between the two oceans was more urgent than ever. If a canal could be cut across the isthmus, it would cut travel time between Puget Sound and the Caribbean by two-thirds.

Britain reluctantly gave the United States the go-ahead to build, control, and fortify a canal. (The Clayton-Bulwer Treaty of 1850 had barred the two countries from obtaining exclusive control over any canal built across the isthmus.) The next question was, Where should the canal be built? Through Nicaragua or through Panama, which was then part of Colombia? The French-owned "New Panama Canal Co." lobbied in Washington for a canal through Panama. It was well served by one of its major stockholders, Philippe Bunau-Varilla, a Frenchman and a most effective lobbyist. The House approved a canal through Panama and authorized the President to secure a right-of-way from Colombia. If he failed, he was required to negotiate with Nicaragua.

Colombia was dissatisfied with Washington's terms and held out for a better offer. At that point the Panamanians, apparently on signal from Bunau-Varilla, staged a rebellion. An hour after President Roosevelt received the news that the Panamanians had declared their independence, he authorized *de facto* recognition of the infant republic.

"The man behind the egg."

Crane. *The New York Times*, 1903.

With Bunau-Varilla representing Panama, the two countries signed a treaty on terms highly favorable to the United States. Panama became virtually an American military outpost.

Roosevelt not only made good his promise to "make the dirt fly" in the isthmus. He also tried to make sure that no European power in the future would have an excuse to interfere with our ships passing through the Caribbean to the canal. In 1904 the Dominican Republic was wracked by civil war, and there was a strong possibility that the island's European creditors might come over and try to make good their investments. This prompted Roosevelt to issue his "corollary" to the Monroe Doctrine. The United States, he declared, henceforth would exercise an international police power in the Western Hemisphere. Anyone who wanted debts collected should apply to Washington.

The World's Constable

Louis Dalrymple. *Judge*, 1905.

47

Outsiders who expected the Latin American republics to object to Roosevelt's "big stick diplomacy" were disappointed. It was not until several years later, when the United States cited the corollary to justify wholesale landings of U. S. Marines in the Caribbean and Central America, that our neighbors protested our strong-arm tactics.

Before he left the White House, President Roosevelt exercised his diplomatic skills yet another time, in Morocco. The Germans and the French were at loggerheads and Europe seemed on the brink of war when Roosevelt talked the powers into a conference. For his peace efforts at Algeciras in 1906 and his mediation at Portsmouth the preceding year, Roosevelt was awarded the Nobel peace prize.

Woodrow Wilson, former president of Princeton University and ex-Governor of New Jersey, was the first Democrat in the White House since 1897. He was an archfoe of imperialism and of war. Yet in his first term he authorized more armed interventions in Latin America than any of his predecessors. Between 1914 and 1916, the United States sent troops into Cuba, Haiti, the Dominican Republic, the Virgin Islands, and Mexico. In 1916 Wilson campaigned on the slogan "He Kept Us Out of War." Only a year later he had the unhappy task of formalizing America's entry into World War I.

When the war exploded in Europe in the summer of 1914, America felt strong, snug, and secure. The vast majority of Americans opposed war. And Wilson's policy of strict neutrality had their blessing. The exceptions were the millions of hyphenated Americans. Pro-Ally and pro-German groups fought bitterly and prodded Washington to take sides.

Out of the Depths

Oscar Edward Cesare. *The Sun* (New York), 1915.

Most Americans remained untouched by the war until the heinous attack on the British passenger ship *Lusitania* by a German submarine off the Irish coast. Among the 1,198 passengers and crew who lost their lives were 128 Americans.

Wilson sent one protest, then another to the Kaiser. Ten months passed before Germany offered to assume liability and pay an indemnity. In the meantime anti-German sentiment grew.

As the war spread across the European continent, most cartoonists actively propagandized for American intervention on the side of England and France.

The Python

Jay N. Darling (Ding). *The Des Moines Register*, c. 1917.

Oscar Cesare of the New York *Sun* was a notable exception. So were the cartoonists on the small, radical, Greenwich Village magazine *The Masses*. One of the most talented, Robert Minor, went on to become editor of the *Daily Worker* and acting head of the American Communist Party. (In 1917 the government suppressed *The Masses* for its belligerent antiwar stand.)

Army Medical Examiner: "At last a perfect soldier!"

Robert Minor. *The Masses,* 1916.

Wilson remained determined to hold to a neutral course and resisted the mounting pressure to join the Allies and help slay "the Beast of Berlin." He made more than one attempt to promote a negotiated peace.

In a memorable address to the Senate in January, 1917, Wilson warned that only "peace without victory" could bring permanent settlement, and he called for a League of Nations. Germany's answer to Wilson's message came at the end of the month: it launched an unrestricted submarine campaign against *all* ships in the war zone. Germany had helped push the United States into war.

How We Forced Germany Into the War

Jay N. Darling. *The Des Moines Register,* c. 1917.

In the interests of preserving our no-alliance tradition, the United States became "associated" with the Allies, rather than allied to them. Allied or associated, the country soon was deeply involved in the war. Over two million Americans saw overseas service. In fact, our fresh manpower helped tip the scales. A year and a half after America's entry, the war ended. The Kaiser was forced to abdicate. An armistice was signed on November 11, 1918.

Nothing Left but the Howl

J. H. Donahey. *The Plain Dealer* (Cleveland), c. 1919.

6

Return to "Normalcy"

On a blustery, cold morning in December, 1918, President Wilson set sail on the *George Washington* to attend the Paris Peace Conference. It was the first visit by an American President to Europe. Wilson's prestige on the Continent had never been greater, but at home his reputation had suffered. In the recent congressional elections, Republicans had captured both houses. Partisan Republicans disapproved of Wilson. They disapproved of his trip. And they disapproved of his Fourteen Points, particularly the fourteenth, calling for a League of Nations. Wilson had outlined Allied war aims in a fourteen-point statement to Congress in January. The address had been widely acclaimed at home and abroad.

Wilson's chief critics in Congress, Senators Borah, Lodge, Reed, and Knox, were convinced that the less truck the United States had with the squabbling European powers, the better off the country would be.

Interrupting the Ceremony

John T. McCutcheon. *The Tribune* (Chicago), 1918.

While Wilson was in Paris, the four senators and their supporters borrowed one of Wilson's principles and exercised their right of "self-determination" as a minority. They served notice on the country and the world that they would approve no peace treaty containing a League Covenant.

The Prescription That Went Astray

Jay N. Darling. *The Des Moines Register,* c. 1919.

When Wilson returned from Paris in February, 1919, he got a mixed reception.

Getting a Taste of It

J. H. Donahey. *The Plain Dealer* (Cleveland), c. 1919.

The League of Nations Argument in a Nutshell

Jay N. Darling. *The Des Moines Register,* c. 1919.

While the President tried to line up congressional support in Washington, the Allies in Paris were putting the finishing touches on the peace treaty. It was signed with great fanfare in the Hall of Mirrors at Versailles on June 28, 1919. As Boardman Robinson foresaw in his prophetic cartoon, the treaty was badly flawed.

Signed

Boardman Robinson. June, 1919.

Discouraged by his failure to convert the "irreconcilables" in the Senate, Wilson left Washington in September, 1919, to take his case for the League and the Versailles Treaty to the country.

Before the month was over, the President collapsed in Pueblo, Colorado. His active campaign for the League was ended.

The Senate continued to debate the League Covenant. Lodge insisted on reservations. Wilson objected: no treaty was preferable to a treaty with reservations. Twice in November, 1919, and again in March, 1920, the Senate voted. Three times it refused to consent to ratification.

The One Animal That Wouldn't Go Into the Ark

Jay N. Darling. *The Des Moines Register,* c. 1920.

The same year that the League was defeated, the country elected Republican Warren Gamaliel Harding President. Harding promised the country a return to "normalcy."

Triumphal Entry Into Normalcy

Rollin Kirby. *The World* (New York), 1921.

The public had mixed feelings about America's not being a League member. Some people were relieved. They considered it an imperfect institution run by quarrelsome, aggressive "foreign imperialists."

John T. McCutcheon. *The Tribune* (Chicago), 1920.

The pro-League internationalists, on the other hand, were irate. If the League was weak, it was due to our failure to join up and make it work.

"We Told You It Wouldn't Work!"

Jay N. Darling. *The Des Moines Register,* c. 1920.

Wilson failed to sell the League to his countrymen, but his vision of America as a moral force in the world working for peace had a lasting impact. Idaho's Senator Borah, the same isolationist who helped defeat the League, persuaded President Harding in November, 1921, to convene the Washington disarmament conference.

The theory behind the conference was, simply, that by eliminating the weapons of war one could eliminate war itself. That struck a responsive chord. When the conference closed, most of the American press and public hailed it as a monument to peace.

Out of the Washington conference came an agreement to stabilize the world's three most powerful navies, the U. S., British, and Japanese, on a capital-ship ratio of 5:5:3. Japan, by agreeing to accept a lower naval ratio, received America's promise not to fortify further any Pacific island except Hawaii.

Our Greatest Naval Victory   **The Roots**

Nelson Harding. *The Brooklyn Daily Eagle*, 1922.   Carey Orr. *The Tribune* (Chicago), c. 1921.

The Hearst papers, representing a vocal minority, deplored the conference results. They claimed that a rapacious Japan was even then formulating secret plans to attack the United States.

Most Americans thought the jingoes were creating a straw dragon to stir up the public over a nonexistent threat.

"It looks fine, but I can't make it breathe!"

Homer Stinson. *Dayton Daily News*, c. 1922.

President Coolidge, the thrifty New Englander who succeeded Harding in 1923, hoped to duplicate his predecessor's disarmament coup and hastily set the stage for a new conference. The 1927 Geneva disarmament conference was a complete failure. France and Italy refused to come. Britain and the United States refused to come to terms.

The Round Trip to the Disarmament Conference

Jay N. Darling. *The Des Moines Register*, 1926.

Undaunted by its failure to outlaw weapons or at least limit them, the United States mounted a campaign to outlaw war itself. With strong public backing, the United States joined sixty-two nations in 1928 in signing the Kellogg-Briand Pact of Paris, renouncing war as "an instrument of national policy." The Senate approved the pact by 85 votes to 1.

Married Again

William A. Ireland. *The Columbus Dispatch*, 1928.

The pact proved to be an illusion. Instead of outlawing war, the treaty merely succeeded in outlawing declarations of war.

Another Blindfold Test

Carey Orr. *The Tribune* (Chicago), 1928.

By 1930 Wilson's hope that World War I would be the "war to end war," a war to make the world "safe for democracy," was looking more and more tenuous.

7

Prelude to Armageddon

The euphoria surrounding the signing of the Kellogg-Briand Pact quickly evaporated. In September, 1931, Japanese troops invaded Manchuria.

The Open Door

Oscar Edward Cesare. *Outlook*, 1931.

Neither the League of Nations nor the signatories of the Pact of Paris were disposed to stop them. The Quaker President, Herbert Hoover, deplored war. With equal vigor he opposed any U. S. involvement. The country sympathized with the Chinese, but the Far East was far away.

The Japanese problem could be ignored but it wouldn't go away. In January, 1932, Japan savagely attacked Shanghai. And in February, at the very moment when the Geneva World Disarmament Conference was meeting, the Japanese set up the puppet state of Manchukuo in Manchuria.

The United States called for diplomatic sanctions. Washington's verbal broadsides carried as much force as a stick of papier-mâché bombs. Within a year Japan announced the Monroe Doctrine of the Orient, or "Asia for the Asiatics." Roughly translated, that meant China for Japan.

Not content with Manchuria, Japanese troops in 1937 marched into northern China. A full-scale Japanese invasion of China was under way, though war was not officially declared until four and a half years later.

The Sleeping Giant Begins to Feel It

Hugh Hutton. *The Philadelphia Inquirer,* 1937.

69

Impressed by Japan's cheap victories in the Far East, Europe's fascist dictators began flexing their muscles. Mussolini brazenly seized Ethiopia late in 1935. Britain and France were agonizing over the prospect of a showdown when Hitler reoccupied the Rhineland.

While the League members smarted from the fresh blows dealt the Versailles Treaty and what was left of the Covenant, Germany and Italy were already deeply embroiled in another campaign, aiding General Francisco Franco's revolt against the Soviet-supported Loyalist government of Spain. In 1936 Hitler and Mussolini formed the anti-Communist Rome-Berlin Axis.

Another Pact

William Gropper, 1936.

Later that same year, Germany and Japan signed a pact. Though they didn't say so, their target was the Soviet Union. Mussolini joined their anti-Communist, antidemocratic alliance the following year.

American Communists denounced the Rome-Berlin-Tokyo Axis.

Labor's Day in Nuremberg

Fred Ellis. *The Daily Worker*, 1937.

A few Americans thought they detected the distant rumblings of another world war. But most of the country turned a deaf ear. Nonintervention was the byword.

In March, 1938, Hitler seized Austria. America was moved—but not moved to act. Britain, though closer to the fire, was no more eager than the United States to put it out.

Too Hungry To Complain

Vaughn Shoemaker, *Chicago Daily News*, 1938.

Hitler's next victim was Czechoslovakia. In the autumn of '38 Hitler demanded the eastern portion of Czechoslovakia, the Sudetenland, whose inhabitants were largely of German descent.

Convinced that war could only be averted by appeasing Hitler, British Prime Minister Chamberlain set off for Munich to meet with French Premier Daladier, Mussolini, and Hitler. The result: a four-power agreement to dismember Czechoslovakia.

Consultation

Grover Page. *The Courier-Journal* (Louisville, Kentucky), 1938.

Chamberlain enjoyed a moment of glory as the man who brought "peace in our time." The moment was short. Instead of an Rx for peace, Munich turned into a witches' brew of war. Not content with half a loaf, Hitler invaded the rest of Czechoslovakia in March, 1939. His next target: Poland.

Sticking His Neck Out

Fred O. Seibel. *Richmond Times-Dispatch,* 1939.

Three obstacles stood in Hitler's path: Britain, France, and the Soviet Union. The first two had capitulated once before, in Munich, and could be expected to do so again. The third, Germany's enemy of long standing, nonaggression pact. Stalin's reward was a share of the booty. The moment was captured in the classic cartoon by the late British cartoonist Sir David Low.

Rendezvous

David Low, 1939.

Hitler had overplayed his hand. On September 3, 1939, two days after the invasion of Poland, Britain and France declared war on Germany. Despite their intervention, Poland fell less than four weeks later.

World War II had begun, but twenty-seven months were to pass before the United States formally entered the struggle against the Axis powers.

8

Blood, Toil, Tears

A Gallup poll taken in October 1939, the month after Britain and France declared war on the Axis, showed that 84 percent of Americans distrusted Hitler and hoped the Allies would win. But an even larger percentage wanted the United States to stay out of war.

**"Come on in. I'll treat you right.
I used to know your Daddy."**

C. D. Batchelor. *Daily News* (New York), 1936.

Isolationists were convinced that the country need never have got involved in 1917 and should certainly not repeat the mistake. From their viewpoint, the "phony war" in Europe was none of Uncle Sam's business—a strictly intramural affair that, as always, victimized Europe's innocents.

To the most zealous isolationists, the campaign against intervention was nothing less than a crusade to save democracy.

The Only Way We Can Save Her

Carey Orr. *The Tribune* (Chicago), 1939.

Those Americans who recognized that our involvement in Europe, no matter how distasteful, was inevitable were a small but growing group. They did not think that the nation could go it alone indefinitely and challenged the isolationists' view that America and Europe were two separate worlds. American Communists, for reasons of their own, wanted the United States to intervene.

The Isolationist

Albert Hirschfeld. *New Masses,* 1938.

In the spring of 1940 Hitler's storm troopers swept across Denmark and Norway. The "phony war" was over. In Britain a new prime minister declared, "I have nothing to offer but blood, toil, tears and sweat."

France fell in June. Britain now stood alone, the last bastion of democracy in Europe.

While the Germans tried to bomb Britain into submission, the interventionists on the other side of the Atlantic demanded action. Roosevelt answered the call. In September he turned over fifty superannuated destroyers to Britain in exchange for eight sites for bases.

In the presidential campaign that fall, both candidates—Roosevelt, who was running for an unprecedented third term, and Wendell Willkie— promised to aid the British and, just as unequivocally, promised to keep the country out of war.

Most Popular Baby of the Campaign

Daniel Robert Fitzpatrick. *St. Louis Post-Dispatch*, 1940.

In January, 1941, Roosevelt made good on one of his campaign pledges. He asked Congress to approve the Lend-Lease Bill. Adolf Hitler lent him a hand.

Support for lend-lease was far from unanimous. Many Americans were suspicious of Roosevelt's intentions. Was lend-lease really "aid short of war" or was it war on the installment plan?

The People Try to Get the White House Viewpoint

Daniel Robert Fitzpatrick. *St. Louis Post-Dispatch*, 1941.

The Lend-Lease Bill carried. America had, in fact, long since abandoned the last vestiges of neutrality. While Roosevelt was considering asking Congress for a declaration of war, the decision was abruptly snatched out of his hands. The Japanese bombs that fell on Pearl Harbor on December 7, 1941, banished partisanship and galvanized the American people. The country was now fully committed to crushing the Axis powers.

The first months of the war were months of defeat and retreat. "The forces endeavoring to enslave the entire world now are moving toward this hemisphere," President Roosevelt told Congress. "Never before has there been a greater challenge to life, liberty and civilization."

In those nightmarish days, German U-boats were sinking American ships faster than new ones were launched. And Japan's Rising Sun engulfed a staggeringly rich empire in the Pacific. Not until November, 1942, was the "end of the beginning" in sight. Allied troops landed in North Africa, the Russians launched their gigantic winter offensive with the encirclement of Stalingrad, and Americans were winning a toehold in the steaming jungles of the Solomons.

Any More?

Lute Pease. *Newark News,* 1942.

British and American cooperation at the summit—if not in the field—had never been closer. Early in 1943 the President flew the Atlantic for the first time to meet Churchill in Casablanca. The Big Two agreed to settle for nothing less than Germany's unconditional surrender.

Der Führer, in predicting an easy victory for the Axis, had grossly miscalculated.

Italy surrendered in September, 1943. The *Vaterland* was under siege. American bombers by day and the RAF by night battered its cities.

While America's relations with Britain continued to get warmer, relations with the "Sphinx of the Kremlin" had become dangerously strained by the late summer of 1943. There was some concern that Stalin might decide to sign a separate peace.

The foreign ministers' conference in Moscow in October, 1943, helped clear the air of Allied differences, and at the end of that year Churchill and Roosevelt, fresh from a meeting with Chiang Kai-shek in Cairo, joined Stalin at the Russian embassy in Teheran. It was the first meeting of the Big Three. They mapped plans for coordinating the Russian offensive against Germany with the opening of a second front. At 6:30 A.M. on June 6, 1944 Allied troops landed on the beaches of Normandy.

Eleven months after D-Day the war in Europe was over. Germany had surrendered.

V for Victory

Bill Crawford. *Newark News,* 1945.

The war in the Pacific had yet to be won. Meeting in a Potsdam palace near Berlin in July, 1945, Stalin, Churchill (later Attlee), and Truman drew up a surrender ultimatum. The Japanese ignored it.

On August 6, the first atomic bomb razed the city of Hiroshima. On August 14, 1945, Japan surrendered.

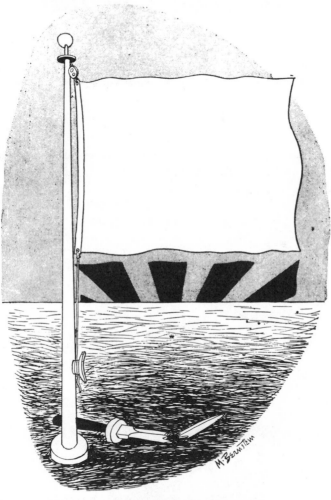

M. Bernstein. *PM*, 1945.

9

The Iron Curtain Descends

The atomic bomb cast an ominous shadow over the postwar world. The only alternative to future chaos, many Americans believed, was international cooperation in One World.

Eventually, Why Not Now?

Jay N. Darling. *The Des Moines Register*, 1945.

Congress, as early as 1943, had voted overwhelmingly to commit the country's support to a world peace organization. A few isolationists remained irreconcilable, but their number had greatly diminished since World War I. By 1945 isolationism was passé. The new fashion in foreign policy was internationalism.

And Company Already Arriving

Jay N. Darling. *The Des Moines Register,* c. 1945.

The ideal of One World, it soon became clear, collided headlong with the reality of postwar politics.

But What Part Shall the Meek Inherit?

Charles G. Werner. *The Indianapolis Star,* 1949.

Churchill, speaking in Fulton, Missouri, in 1946, warned of an "iron curtain" descending on Europe.

In an atmosphere of mounting tension the Allied foreign ministers met late in 1945 and again in 1946 to negotiate peace terms with Hungary, Rumania, Bulgaria, Finland, and Italy. The American public did not care for the results. Secretary of State Byrnes, they objected, had been too conciliatory to Foreign Minister Molotov and his boss.

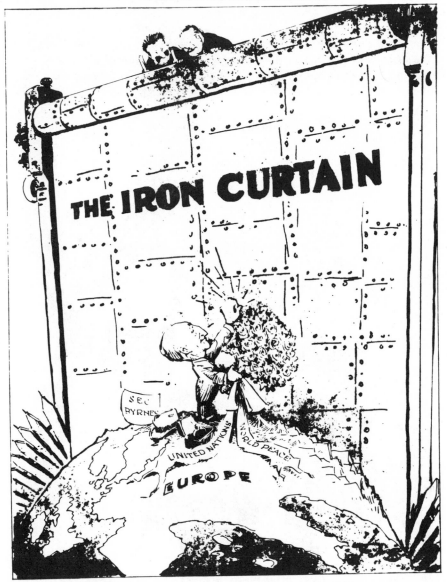

Jay N. Darling. *The Des Moines Register,* c. 1946.

Hungary, Rumania, and Bulgaria enjoyed only brief independence. Contrary to the Yalta agreement of February, 1945, free elections were never held in Eastern Europe. And one by one the governments were subverted to communism. The arrangements made at Yalta and at Potsdam in the summer of 1945 governing Germany were also coming unstuck. Under the agreements, Germany had been divided into four occupation zones.

Nobody Is Happy

Burt R. Thomas. *The Detroit News,* 1949.

The war had ravaged the economies of the Western European nations. If they didn't get some stiff medicine quickly, the illness could prove fatal.

Great Expectations

Edwin Marcus. *The New York Times,* 1947.

America's answer to Stalin's iron-curtain diplomacy was the Truman Doctrine. When the rightist Greek government was threatened by Communist guerrillas early in 1947, America rushed to the rescue with a $400 million emergency aid program. "It must be the policy of the United States," Truman told Congress, "to support free peoples who are resisting attempted subjugation . . ." The "containment" policy was launched.

The Truman Doctrine was the precursor of the vastly more ambitious and costly Marshall Plan. In December, 1947, Truman asked Congress for $17 billion for a four-year program to spur Western Europe's economic recovery. For three long months Congress debated while Europe waited.

Step on it, Doc!

Roy Justus. *The Minneapolis Star*, 1947.

Backers of the plan argued that a healthy Europe was vital to America's future well-being. Opponents called it "Operation Rathole." Europe, if it put its mind to it, could recover without the help of "Uncle Santa Claus."

The most adamant opposition to the European Recovery Program, as the Marshall Plan was formally called, came from the isolationists. They wanted America to tend to its own knitting.

Some Day They'll Come Crawling Back to Her

Joseph Parrish. *The Tribune* (Chicago), 1949.

Stalin inadvertently gave the Marshall Plan's supporters a hand. In February, 1948, a Communist coup, which was followed by the "suicide" of Foreign Minister Masaryk, brought Czechoslovakia under the Soviet heel.

The shock helped swing the undecided votes in Congress over to the aid program. By mid-'48 most of the country favored a "get tough with Stalin" policy.

Berlin was the scene of the next crisis in Soviet-American relations. Just as Truman and New York's Republican Governor Thomas E. Dewey were hitting the campaign trail, the Russians blocked the land routes to Berlin. Britain and the United States broke the blockade with a mammoth airlift that lasted almost a year. Not only did Stalin fail to take Berlin but he helped scare the Marshall Plan countries into a military alliance.

Unintentional Cupid

Richard Q. Yardley. *The Sun* (Baltimore), 1949.

For the United States, the North Atlantic Treaty was a major break with tradition. Never before in peacetime had America signed a formal treaty of alliance with a European power. The Senate approved NATO in 1949 with few dissenting votes.

Putting teeth into the alliance presented a greater problem for a cost-conscious Congress. But convinced as we were that Stalin meant to "bury" us, we saw no alternative. By 1950 the United States had demonstrated its determination to keep Stalin out of the free world.

An Increasingly Difficult Neighborhood

Dan Dowling. *New York Herald Tribune,* 1950.

93

10

Two Generals and the Man from Independence, Mo.

While America and its NATO allies were securing their Eastern European flank, a major upheaval was under way on the other side of the globe. The "China problem" had been simmering on the State Department's back burner since 1945. The end of the war found Chiang Kai-shek's Nationalists and Mao Tse-tung's Communists at each other's throats. U. S. troops gave Chiang Kai-shek logistical help in '45 and then headed home.

Prisoner of War

M. Bernstein. *PM*, 1945.

Late that year General Marshall made a trip to China, hoping to help the two sides iron out their differences. But the negotiations fell through.

In 1948 the Chinese Communists overran Manchuria. The Nationalists began to crumble. Republicans urged Truman to go to Chiang's rescue, but Truman demurred. A white paper released in August, 1949, stated that if the Nationalists collapsed, they had no one to blame but themselves.

How Long?

Paule Loring. *The Evening Bulletin* (Providence), 1949.

95

Four months later the Communists drove Chiang and his troops from the mainland to Taiwan (Formosa). The Russian bear, or so it seemed to the authorities in Washington at the time, was in complete control of the Chinese dragon.

Hard to Recognize

Burt R. Thomas. *The Detroit News,* 1949.

While the Administration was fending off Republican attacks for "losing" China, the most serious crisis since the war was in the making. On June 25, 1950, the Russian-trained and -equipped North Korean army invaded South Korea.

Starting Something?

Edwin Marcus. *The New York Times*, 1950.

That same day the UN Security Council met and, in the absence of the Soviet delegate, named North Korea the aggressor. On June 27, the Council called on its members for military assistance, and the President ordered air and naval forces into Korea. Two days later, Truman authorized ground troops.

By the end of the year UN forces—chiefly Americans together with small contingents from fifteen other countries—had repulsed the invaders and driven them back across the 38th parallel into North Korea. Suddenly Chinese "volunteers" entered the war. They promptly hurled the UN forces back across the border.

China's intervention changed the scope of the war. It also changed Americans' attitudes. A Gallup poll taken in January, 1951, showed that two out of three Americans wanted us to pull out of Korea altogether. Why should we fight somebody else's war?

Others felt that the only answer to the Communist onslaught was a fight to the finish. They agreed with General MacArthur that "There is no substitute for victory" and that the place to win a victory was on the battlefield, not at the negotiating table.

Hemmed In

Reg Manning, 1951.

"Mr. Truman's war," as the Republicans called it, loomed large in the presidential campaign of 1952. The foreign policy of Truman and his Secretary of State, Dean Acheson, struck a sour note with the public.

General Eisenhower promised, if elected, to make a personal trip to Korea. The five-star general won the election by a landslide. He made his promised trip in December. In July, 1953, an armistice was signed which provided for a cease-fire on existing battle lines and a political conference to settle the peace terms.

The Korean war was a blow to America's self-esteem. Fighting for a draw rather than all-out victory rankled. President Eisenhower promised that in the future the United States would seize the offensive in the cold war. We would not merely contain communism; we would liberate its victims.

For openers, the United States "unleashed" Chiang Kai-shek to make raids on the mainland. (Up to that time the remnants of his army on Taiwan had been neutralized by the U. S. Seventh Fleet.) We also showered him with economic and military aid. Critics of the Administration felt the military assistance was excessive. They warned that we were making a commitment that might ultimately embroil us in war with the mainland.

"And the best part is that *he's* paying *us* for the ride."

Bill Mauldin. *St. Louis Post-Dispatch*, 1958.
Copyright 1958—St. Louis Post-Dispatch.
Reproduced by courtesy of Bill Mauldin.

It was the Communists, not the Nationalists, who triggered a war scare in 1958, when they shelled two tiny Nationalist-held island groups, Quemoy and Matsu, just off the coast. About a third of Chiang's forces were stationed on the island outposts. He could have used the bombardment as an excuse to attempt his long-awaited "return to the mainland." But Secretary of State Dulles dissuaded him. Washington was unwilling to risk a full-scale fight.

"Let's You and Him Fight."

Richard Q. Yardley. *The Sun* (Baltimore), c. 1958.

The Administration abandoned liberation in favor of a middle course. The United States agreed to help defend the Quemoy and Matsu islands if the need arose. In turn it extracted a promise from the Nationalists not to use force to regain the mainland. Chiang was now back on the leash.

The timing of the Chinese Communist bombardment of the tiny islands in 1958 was no accident. The United States at that moment was wrestling with another crisis in a different part of the world, the Middle East.

Ever since 1955, when the Russians made an arms-and-aid deal with Egypt's Nasser, the United States had agonized over Soviet inroads in the area. Yet in 1956, when Britain, France, and Israel attacked Egypt, the United States had joined Russia in insisting they withdraw. (Britain and France were retaliating against Nasser for nationalizing the Suez Canal.) The United States lost no love over Nasser, but it didn't approve of the use of force—a flagrant violation of the UN Charter.

Nasser came out of the fight with his control of the Suez intact, while what was left of British influence in the Mediterranean was destroyed.

Britain's retreat left a dangerous power vacuum in the oil-rich Middle East. The Russians were eager to fill it.

Demonstration on Filling a Vacuum

John R. Stampone. *The Army Times,* 1956.

Eisenhower served notice that the vacuum would not be filled without a struggle. In January, 1957, he had asked Congress for authority to supply military and economic aid to any Communist-threatened country in the Middle East that requested it. Some Democrats twitted the Administration for reverting to Truman's now unfashionable containment policy.

"Well, It's Sort Of New With Us"

Herbert L. Block (Herblock). *The Washington Post,* 1957.
From *Herblock's Special For Today* (Simon & Schuster, 1958)

But enough Democrats went along with the Republicans to assure passage of the "Eisenhower Doctrine."

Not As Impossible As It May Seem

Ed Valtman. *The Hartford Times*, 1956.

The Eisenhower Doctrine was put to the test in the summer of 1958, when the pro-Western king of Iraq was murdered. A power grab by Nasser seemed imminent. Lebanon at the time was plagued by internal disorders and was afraid of becoming Egypt's next punching bag after Iraq. Beirut appealed to Washington for help.

Mideast Tableau

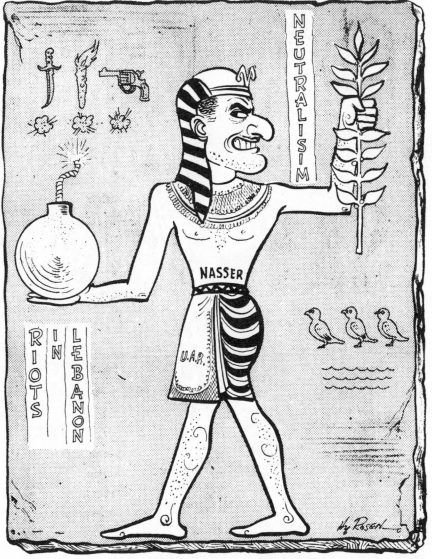

Hy Rosen. *The Times-Union* (Albany), 1958.

The Marines landed in Lebanon the day after the coup in Iraq. The Russians warned Washington that it was approaching the "brink of disaster." But the Marines stood their ground. And the UN's Arab members, in a dramatic about-face, promised not to interfere in each other's internal affairs. The United States pulled out its troops in October, mission accomplished, and the East-West competition in the Middle East reverted to the less provocative form of aid and trade.

Cleopatra

Warren King. *Daily News* (New York), 1959.

11

The Summit Syndrome

Throughout the Eisenhower years, the Russians alternated saber-rattling with the soft sell. After Stalin's death in 1953, Malenkov launched his "peace offensive." Many Americans were skeptical about his true intentions.

But How About the Basic Design!

John Milt Morris. AP Newsfeatures, 1953.

Malenkov was forced to resign in 1955, and Khrushchev took his turn at the peace game. He coaxed a reluctant Eisenhower to join him at a summit meeting in Geneva. The "spirit of Geneva" turned out to be exactly that—all vapor, no substance.

The Cheshire Cat

Scott Long. *The Minneapolis Tribune*, 1955.

In the mid-'50s the United States felt confident of its military and technological superiority. That conviction was badly shaken in the fall of 1957. On October 4 the Russians orbited the world's first man-made earth satellite.

Moscow called for another summit meeting. This time Washington declined. Any lingering doubts about the sincerity of the Soviet Union's peace drive were laid to rest in November, 1958, by Khrushchev's ultimatum on Berlin. Unless the other three occupying powers agreed to make Berlin a "free city," he declared, within six months the Russians would turn over control of their sector to the East Germans.

Hardly two months had passed when the Russians abruptly changed their tune. The Berlin deadline expired without incident, and there was a new thaw in U. S.-Soviet relations. Once more Moscow issued a call for a heads-of-state meeting. Some Kremlinologists believed a Soviet-American tête-à-tête couldn't hurt and might even help the cause of peace. Eisenhower agreed, and he invited Khrushchev over for a visit in September. The Soviet leader's trip was greeted with restrained optimism.

Herbert L. Block. *The Washington Post,* 1959.
From *Straight Herblock* (Simon & Schuster, 1964)

After a speech to the United Nations and a cross-country tour, Khrushchev joined Eisenhower at Camp David. The two leaders agreed to a follow-up meeting in May in Paris.

As May, 1960, approached, Khrushchev once again turned bellicose and threatened to sign a separate peace treaty with East Germany. Eleven days before the conference was to convene, the Soviet leader dropped a bombshell. Gary Powers' U-2 spy plane had been shot down on an espionage mission over Soviet territory. The Russians used the incident to scuttle the summit meeting. At the same time they scored a resounding propaganda victory.

In June the Soviet delegation walked out of the Geneva disarmament talks. The attacks on the United States grew more strident. In September Khrushchev moved the show to New York and the General Assembly. For twenty-five days he heaped threats and insults on the United States and the other Western "colonialists." His performance was designed to impress the growing Afro-Asian bloc. But it backfired.

Bill Mauldin. *St. Louis Post-Dispatch,* 1960.
Copyright 1960—St. Louis Post-Dispatch.
Reproduced by courtesy of Bill Mauldin.

A number of prominent neutral UN delegates tried to bring Eisenhower and Khrushchev together. But the President declined. He had learned the hard way the perils of summitry.

"... And there's a bad crevasse just past this ridge ..."

Bill Mauldin. *St. Louis Post-Dispatch*, 1961.
Copyright 1961—St. Louis Post-Dispatch.
Reproduced by courtesy of Bill Mauldin.

Khrushchev pressed for a summit conference after the presidential elections, but neither of the candidates, Vice President Nixon and Senator John F. Kennedy, would commit himself. Both seemed to agree that summit meetings were best avoided unless the foundations were laid at less lofty levels.

A major issue in the campaign of 1960 was the relative strength of the U. S. and Soviet strategic nuclear forces. Kennedy charged that the Republicans had underestimated Soviet military capabilities and allowed the country to fall behind in the nuclear arms race. Russia's widely touted space triumphs lent credibility to his charges.

The vaunted "missile gap" turned out to be an illusion. The experts had miscalculated.

**"Now This Is the Gissile Map,
I Mean Gappile Miss, I Mean . . ."**

Hank Barrow. *The Omaha World-Herald,* 1961.

Retracting the missile-gap allegations was the least of the new President's worries. When he took office in January, 1961, Kennedy found his desk buried in the cold-war fallout of Berlin and Cuba. His first hundred days were tainted by the disastrous attempted invasion of Cuba at the Bay of Pigs; his next hundred, by Khrushchev's new ultimatum on Berlin. The Soviet cold warrior apparently believed the novice in the White House lacked backbone.

"Kennedy back trouble is big capitalist lie.
Secret X-ray intelligence
shows is having no spine!"

Charles G. Werner. *The Indianapolis Star*, 1961.

Far from bowing to the Soviet threat, Kennedy asked Congress for authority to call up 250,000 reservists. "We do not want to fight," Kennedy told the nation in July, "but we have fought before."

Soviet frustration over the failure of their bullying tactics was compounded by the embarrassing outpouring of refugees from the East German "workers' paradise." In August, without warning, the Communists erected a wall of concrete and barbed wire between East and West Berlin to stanch the flow.

"See how many are staying on our side."

Don Wright. *The Miami News*, 1961.

The next Soviet challenge was closer to home. In 1962 Soviet oil, arms, and technicians flowed into Cuba, ninety miles off the Florida coast. Some Administration critics called for a blockade, others for the invasion of Cuba. Russian intervention in the Caribbean, they argued, violated the time-honored Monroe Doctrine and must be stopped.

A Doctrine Discuss'd

Richard Q. Yardley. *The Sun* (Baltimore), 1962.

The Administration favored restraint. Then in mid-October, 1962, aerial photographs revealed that Soviet technicians were stationing nuclear missiles with a range of over one thousand miles in Cuba. The United States faced one of the gravest decisions in history: retreat, or stand fast and risk a nuclear showdown.

Showdown

Warren King. *Daily News* (New York), 1962.

On October 22, the President went on television to announce that he was quarantining all ships carrying offensive weapons to Cuba. A quarantine was tantamount to a blockade, and a blockade was an act of war. Would the Russians realize we weren't bluffing? Would they back down?

"I'd Reconsider If I Were You!"

Richard Q. Yardley. *The Sun* (Baltimore), 1962.

As an anxious world waited, the news broke that the Russian ships which had been steaming toward Cuba on collision course had turned back. On October 28, Khrushchev agreed to withdraw his offensive weapons from America's back door.

Retreat

Hy Rosen, *The Times-Union* (Albany), 1962.

The United States had weathered the most dangerous confrontation of the cold war.

12

*Alliances
in Disarray*

Although it would be some time before most Americans recognized the
fact, trouble was brewing in the Communist world. The Soviet Union was
still going through the motions of demanding Red China's admission to the
United Nations, but its heart was not really in it.

The Girl He Left Behind

Ed Holland. *The Tribune* (Chicago), 1960.

A rift had developed between the two Communist giants. By 1960 the Russians had recalled their scientists and technicians and suspended their nuclear aid to China. In time the split came out into the open. Moscow and Peking hurled insults at each other. Both tried to woo the uncommitted Third World. In late 1963 Chou En-lai began a grand tour of Africa.

"... And you, what would you like for Christmas?"

Burges Green. *The Providence Journal*, 1963.

While Khrushchev called for peaceful coexistence with the West and castigated Maoist adventurism, the Chinese were pushing a hard, revolutionary line and denouncing Soviet "revisionism."

"Stop Enjoying Yourself."

Guernsey LePelley. *The Christian Science Monitor*, 1964.

"Forward!"

John Fischetti, 1964.

Red China accused Khrushchev of having gone soft on imperialism. Khrushchev was not about to take such charges lying down and decided to have a showdown with China at a meeting of world Communist parties. His enthusiasm for a showdown was not shared, and in October, 1964, Khrushchev suddenly found himself out of power and out of work.

The new Soviet leaders tried to patch up relations with Peking. They didn't get very far. Emboldened by the explosion of its first nuclear device the very day of Khrushchev's ouster, Peking was trying to recruit Communist allies. It suffered one rebuff after another. The greatest blow of all was the overthrow of the pro-Peking Communists in Indonesia in 1965.

". . . Drunk? . . . Of course I'm not drunk!!"

Paul Conrad. *The Los Angeles Times,* 1965.

If the United States had not been having its own difficulties with its democratic partners, it might have taken comfort from the disarray in the Communist world. There was a serious rift in the North Atlantic alliance, and Washington's efforts to paper over the cracks had so far failed. A frustrated Administration blamed the failure, or a large part of it, on France's strong-willed and independent President, Charles de Gaulle.

The friction between the French general and the United States went back to World War II. De Gaulle, leader of the Free French, felt snubbed by Roosevelt. "*Les américains,*" he claimed, had sold France short.

Clifford K. Berryman. *Washington Star,* 1944.

When De Gaulle moved into the Elysée Palace in 1958, many Americans felt he could give France what it needed most after a rapid succession of unstable governments—a firm hand at the tiller. After setting the country on a steady course, De Gaulle turned to the task of proving that France was still a great power. Since nuclear capability and great-power status seemed inseparable, he insisted that France build its own *force de frappe* (nuclear force).

Kennedy's "Grand Design" envisaged an Atlantic partnership linking the United States and Canada with a united Europe. But De Gaulle had different ideas. He favored a loosely associated "Europe of States" totally independent of the Americans. The federation would be led either by France alone or by France in collaboration with a nonnuclear Germany.

The idea of a Franco-German entente appealed to Chancellor Adenauer. His successor, Ludwig Erhard, thought it wiser to cultivate the American connection.

"I'm here, Ludwig . . . Have no fear!"

Pierre Bellocq (Peb). *The Philadelphia Inquirer*, 1964.

By judicious bargaining, Bonn hoped to persuade Washington to give Germany a greater say over NATO's nuclear strategy.

"How much ist das bombie in das vindow?"

Gene Basset, c. 1965.

The United States was willing to explore the matter, but approval would be conditional on Germany and the other NATO allies picking up a greater share of the defense costs.

While Washington was mulling the matter over, De Gaulle dropped his "bomb." At a 1965 press conference, he announced France's decision to "end the subordination known as 'integration' which is provided for by NATO." By 1969 at the latest France would withdraw from the integrated military command structure.

**"If you won't play my way
I'll take my ball and go home."**

Hugh Haynie. *The Courier-Journal* (Louisville, Kentucky), 1965.
(A careful look at Haynie's cartoons
reveals the name of his wife, Lois.)

A few months later De Gaulle told the American troops and other NATO forces stationed in France to pack up and get out.

The Adamant Concierge

Richard Q. Yardley. *The Sun* (Baltimore), 1966.

The cause of North Atlantic unity had suffered a major setback.

13

Five Hens and the Gallic Rooster

America's difficulties with Le Grand Charles were minor compared to those of Britain. London wanted to join the thriving European Economic Community, or Common Market, but Paris's answer had been "*Non*" in 1963, and it was still "*Non*" in 1967.

"It's Not THAT Common!"

Ray Osrin. *The Plain Dealer* (Cleveland), 1967.

De Gaulle preferred the Common Market the way it was, a "barnyard with five hens and one Gallic rooster." He didn't consider Britain continental and he mistrusted its special relationship with the United States. Let in a few Anglo-Saxons and before long they would be bringing their friends and trying to take over. As it was, France considered America's presence in Europe excessive.

When Britain received its second rebuff from the Elysée Palace, Americans' sympathies were with Harold Wilson, the rejected suitor. De Gaulle had not only rejected Britain's application only five days after it was formally submitted, but he raked the country over the coals.

**"Before we take you into our club
the Membership Committee has a few questions."**

Robert Bastian. *San Francisco Chronicle*, 1967.

De Gaulle cast his third and last veto in 1968. Economically, Britain was a basket case, according to De Gaulle. It suffered from chronic balance-of-payments deficits and a hopeless pound sterling. Germany and the other members did not agree and wanted Britain in.

"Forget It, Messieurs, Nothing Can Be Done."

Pierre Bellocq, *The Philadelphia Inquirer*, 1968.

The United States had been an early booster of the Common Market. In 1958, when the Six set up a customs union and agreed to adopt a common external tariff, the United States applauded the move. We realized it would mean greater economic competition, but at the time we had a healthy trade surplus. Although our balance of payments was in the red, we weren't too alarmed.

By 1968 the picture had changed. The cost of supporting military forces in Europe and fighting a war in Southeast Asia, not to mention foreign aid and overseas investments, added up to a mounting deficit in our balance of payments. Our trade surplus was shrinking, and confidence in the dollar abroad was slipping rapidly.

Rightly or wrongly, many Americans blamed the Common Market for most of our trade woes. If the Common Market expanded to include Britain, it might strengthen the Atlantic alliance but it might also add to our trade difficulties by reenforcing the competition.

"Doc, my heart's fine, but I keep getting this pain in my wallet . . ."

C. Sanford Huffaker. *The News and Observer* (Raleigh, North Carolina), 1971.

The protectionists in the country were making a comeback. In November, 1970, the House of Representatives approved a highly restrictive trade bill. The United States, it appeared, was about to abandon its free-trade policy.

The bill died with the 91st Congress, but protectionist sentiment was far from dead.

By August, 1971, our gold reserves were perilously low and, for the first time in this century, the country faced the prospect that its imports might exceed exports. President Nixon's solution was a "New Economic Policy." He devalued the dollar and suspended the dollar's convertibility into gold.

"More Gum, Connally—And Get A Longer Stick"

Don Wright. *The Miami News*, 1971.

The President also slapped a temporary 10 percent surcharge on all dutiable imports. Opponents denounced the new policy: they called it an inflammatory provocation of our trade partners, and warned we should expect retaliation in kind.

The industrialized nations did protest. But the Administration was not moved. It countered with the charge that our trading partners imposed more restrictions on U. S. exports and investment than we imposed on theirs.

"Take It Off! Take It All Off!!"

Pat Oliphant. *The Denver Post*, 1971.

Protectionists recalled that not so long ago Western Europe and Japan had been prostrate and the United States had helped them back on their feet. Now that they had fully recovered, they were trying to price us out of the market.

A major reason why Washington had supported European integration from the outset, despite the economic problems it presented, was political. It would strengthen North Atlantic unity and, it was hoped, reduce the likelihood of war between East and West. By 1969 that hope seemed to be paying off. NATO's Communist counterpart, the Warsaw Pact, cautiously proposed an all-European security conference. In December NATO agreed.

"And to think I set him up in business!"

Gib Crockett. *Washington Star,* 1971.

Ray Osrin. *The Plain Dealer* (Cleveland), 1969.

By mid-1971 the Soviet Union was offering to discuss troop reductions. NATO again was receptive. And so were many Americans who had been trying to persuade the Administration to do just that—bring back some of our boys from Europe and save the taxpayers' money. The Administration was unalterably opposed: a 50 percent reduction in U. S. forces in Europe, which Senator Mansfield was advocating, would be "precipitous" and "drastic" and would "destroy all confidence in NATO." Supporters of the Mansfield amendment claimed we were carrying a disproportionate share of Europe's defense burden. But they were outvoted 61–36.

"I'll carry the bar . . ."

Robert Graysmith. *San Francisco Chronicle*, 1971.

Nixon was not opposed to burden sharing, but what he had in mind was persuading NATO to cover 100 percent of the foreign-exchange cost of keeping our forces on the Continent. The implication that they weren't carrying their load didn't sit well with our allies. Nor did the general drift of U. S. foreign policy in 1972. That year Nixon made his historic visit to Peking and exchanged toasts with Brezhnev in Moscow. Western Europe felt neglected. In an effort to let Europe know we still cared, we announced that 1973 would be the Year of Europe. The year came and went without any discernible improvement in Atlantic relations.

"It's From Europe. They're Thinking About Having A 'Year Of The United States.'"

Herbert L. Block. *The Washington Post,* 1974.
Copyright 1974 by Herblock in The Washington Post

14

Vietnam: Tragedy in Five Acts

Europe had reason to feel neglected. The neglect was partly deliberate, partly the result of Washington's preoccupation with Indochina. Not only did our NATO allies not lend us a hand in Vietnam, but some stood on the sidelines and criticized.

President Johnson sent the first U. S. combat troops to South Vietnam in 1965 to prevent a Communist takeover.

"We've got to operate, and fast!"

Pierre Bellocq. *The Philadelphia Inquirer*, 1965.

However, that was by no means the beginning of our direct involvement in Vietnam. President Eisenhower had supplied military aid to Saigon, and President Kennedy had sent in military "advisers."

The Johnson Administration stated that the survival of the government of South Vietnam was vital to our national interests and to world peace. Since there had been a succession of governments following President Diem's ouster in 1963, it was not always clear exactly whom or what we were defending.

"The pattern as a whole is undecipherable; the brain becomes confused and the total effect is quite maddening!"

Frank Interlandi. *The Los Angeles Times,* 1965.

The decision to send G.I.'s into battle on the other side of the globe was controversial, to say the least. Newspaper pundits were of different minds. Walter Lippmann believed the United States was fighting "an impossible war in an impossible environment . . . committed to an unattainable objective." Joseph Alsop called for a greater U. S. military commitment.

"Dr. Lippmann wants to amputate, but Dr. Alsop says to take more shots."

Bill Mauldin. *The Sun-Times* (Chicago), 1965.
Copyright 1965—Chicago Sun-Times. Reproduced by courtesy of
Wil-Jo Associates, Inc., and Bill Mauldin.

The public was deeply divided. Antiwar activists called the war immoral. Administration supporters claimed that antiwar agitators were playing directly into the hands of the enemy.

Correspondents reported that U. S. forces were using tear gas. The Pentagon explained that the gas was nonlethal and a humane weapon. But many Americans were shocked.

"Not an effective gas? . . . It caused nausea and tears as far away as the State Department."

Isadore J. Parker. *The Washington Post,* 1965.

Despite fresh infusions of men and weapons, the war continued to go badly. Villages that government troops liberated by day were reoccupied by Vietcong guerrillas at night. To stop the erosion of Saigon's control of the countryside, Washington beefed up its economic assistance.

"Could you point out the ground you've taken? We're here to secure and develop it economically."

Pat Oliphant. *The Denver Post*, 1966.

As the months wore on, peace did not seem any closer. The United States had three choices: go all out to win, get out, or hang in there.

The Strategists

Bill Mauldin. *The Sun-Times* (Chicago), 1966.
Copyright 1966—Chicago Sun Times. Reproduced by courtesy of
Wil-Jo Associates, Inc., and Bill Mauldin.

In the face of mounting criticism, President Johnson reiterated that the United States had a commitment to defend South Vietnam's freedom. He would see the commitment through—even if it hurt.

David Levine. *The New York Review of Books*, 1966.

As opponents of the war demonstrated, prayed, burned, bombed, and fasted, Senator Fulbright and other "doves" in the Senate challenged the legality of the "President's war." They accused the President of misleading them when he asked them to support the Tonkin Gulf resolution back in August, 1964.

"Only Thing We're Sure Of—There Is a Tonkin Gulf!"

Bil Canfield. *Star-Ledger* (Newark), 1968.

The "hawks" were also down on Johnson. By opposing what he called "mindless escalation," the President was following a no-win strategy, they charged.

Middle Course

Cal Alley. *The Commercial Appeal* (Memphis, Tennessee), 1968.

In March, 1968, several months before the presidential election, Johnson announced he would not be a candidate. He simultaneously announced the suspension of American bombing raids over North Vietnam and renewed his call for peace talks. Negotiations finally got under way in Paris in May.

The Johnsons retired to the LBJ Ranch in January, 1969, and the Nixons moved into the White House. The light at the end of the tunnel was still barely visible. In July Nixon flew to Guam and outlined the "Nixon Doctrine." It was a compromise between total commitment and total disengagement. He called for the "Vietnamization" of the war and the phased withdrawal of U. S. troops (which had reached a wartime peak of 550,000 in 1969). At the same time, he asked Congress to approve a draft by lottery.

"Happy birthday to youuuu . . . Happy birthday to . . ."

Wayne Stayskal. *Chicago Today*, 1969.

Although the American public didn't know it, U. S. planes began bombing Cambodia in 1969. In the spring of 1970 American ground forces crossed the border into Cambodia.

"I never did say how, but I told you I'd get you out of Vietnam."

John Fischetti. *Chicago Daily News*, 1970.

Their mission was to clear out sanctuaries used by the Vietcong and North Vietnamese in waging war in South Vietnam. If the Communist bases and supply depots were still there, our troops didn't find them.

"No, Hanson, You Didn't Find a Box of Bullets and Two Bags of Rice. You Captured an Ammo Dump and a Supply Depot."

Bill Mauldin. *The Sun-Times* (Chicago), 1970.
Copyright 1970—Chicago Sun Times. Reproduced by courtesy of
Wil-Jo Associates, Inc., and Bill Mauldin.

Washington was also concerned over the North Vietnamese buildup in Laos. Early in 1970 B-52's began bombing Pathet Lao positions.

It became necessary to destroy (a) South Vietnam, (b) Laos, (c) Cambodia, (d) Thailand, (e) all of the above—to save Southeast Asia.

Paul Conrad. *The Los Angeles Times,* 1970.

The following year the Administration confirmed it was supporting a thirty-thousand-man "irregular" force in Laos.

"Come on out, Richard—We know you're in there!"

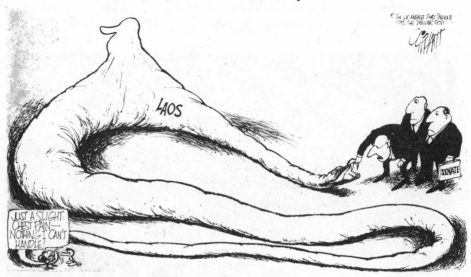

Pat Oliphant. *The Denver Post,* 1971.

During 1971 the air war was intensified as the United States continued to pull out its ground combat forces from South Vietnam. The Administration had ordered a resumption of the bombing raids on North Vietnam in December, 1970—the first since the 1968 halt. The President called the attacks "protective reaction strikes" prompted by North Vietnamese attacks on unarmed U. S. reconnaissance planes.

Doonesbury

Garry B. Trudeau, 1972.

In March, 1972, thousands of North Vietnamese crossed the Demilitarized Zone into South Vietnam. In May the Navy mined the harbor of Haiphong.

Less than two weeks before the election, on October 26, 1972, Dr. Kissinger told a news conference he believed that "peace is at hand" in Indochina. But the secret negotiations between Kissinger and the North Vietnamese, which had begun in August, 1969, broke down. In December the war again escalated. The U. S. bombing of North Vietnam that month was the heaviest of the war.

By the time the Agreement Ending the War and Restoring the Peace in Vietnam was signed on January 27, 1973, some 56,000 Americans had died; 1,359 were "missing in action." For the time being, at least, the United States had "saved" South Vietnam and President Thieu's government, but many Americans believed the price had been too high.

Snow White and the Seven Experiments

Corky Trinidad. *Honolulu Star-Bulletin*, 1970.

The signing of the agreement did not signal the end of the war. President Ford had hardly settled into the White House following President Nixon's resignation in August, 1974, when he was asking Congress to vote enough military and economic aid to make good our commitments to our allies in South Vietnam . . .

"Anyone care to give again to Vietnam . . . ?"

Pat Oliphant. *The Denver Post,* 1975.

and to our allies in Cambodia. . . .

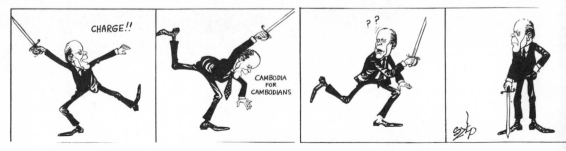

Paul Szep. *The Boston Globe,* 1975.
(Szep weaves his wife's name, Ann, into his cartoons.)

By early 1975 the American public's attitude toward aid for Southeast Asia had hardened. In Congress the President's pleas for additional military assistance encountered firm opposition.

Cambodia fell to the Khmer Rouge in April, '75. South Vietnam's fall was imminent when Dobbins drew the "End of the Domino Theory." Ding's World War I python symbolizing German military power was reincarnated as a Communist viper.

End of the Domino Theory

James J. Dobbins. *Boston Herald-American*, 1975.

15

The Odd Couple: Soviet-American Détente

The Vietnam war had been a major source of friction between the United States and the Soviet Union. Another, much older source was the arms race. The United States emerged from World War II with a monopoly over atomic energy. It offered to place its atomic weapons and know-how under international control, but the Russians weren't interested. They wanted us to destroy our bombs first and discuss controls later. Unable to see eye to eye, the two countries spent billions trying to make certain they were unbeatable.

The Nixon Administration didn't invent the arms race; it inherited it. Not long after he was sworn in, the President announced that his goal was nuclear weapons "sufficiency." He defined "sufficiency" to include an antiballistic missile (ABM) defense system. ABM, he explained, would serve a dual function: it would protect the country against Chinese attack, and it would strengthen our hand in arms-control negotiations.

Despite the Administration's insistence that an ABM system was vital to the nation's security and diplomatic credibility, some people remained skeptical.

"You Against Protection or Something?"

Bil Canfield. *Star-Ledger* (Newark), 1969.

Senate foes of ABM lost in a close vote. It was the second defeat in 1969 for critics of the Administration's arms policy. Earlier in the year, thirty-nine Senators backed a ban on the testing of MIRVs—multiple independently targetable reentry vehicles. They were afraid MIRVs would further destabilize the arms race. But they were outvoted, and the testing began.

"As Soon As Mirv Is Ready He'll Go To The Conference With You."

Herbert L. Block. *The Washington Post*, 1969.
Copyright 1969 by Herblock in The Washington Post

MIRVs were one of the hottest items on the agenda of the strategic arms limitation talks (SALT) between the United States and the Soviet Union.

"Gentlemen, the main course is getting hot!"

Robert Graysmith. *San Francisco Chronicle,* 1969.

After preliminary discussions in Helsinki in November, 1969, serious negotiations began in Vienna early in 1970. The United States was clearly ahead in numbers of submarine-launched ballistic missiles. The Soviet Union held the lead in the number of land-based missiles. The one thing the two sides had in common, apparently, was a genuine interest in some kind of agreement.

"Do Me A Favor—Help Me Drop It!"

Pat Oliphant. *The Denver Post,* 1970.

Throughout 1970 and again in 1971 the SALT talks alternated between Helsinki and Vienna. At home, Deputy Defense Secretary Packard made a pitch for more missiles. They were essential "bargaining chips" for our negotiators. Administration critics wondered whether both sides didn't already have more than enough.

Ranan Lurie, 1970.

Rumors of a breakthrough in the talks were confirmed at the
Nixon-Brezhnev summit meeting in Moscow. There, in the Great Hall of
the Kremlin, on May 26, 1972, the two leaders signed a Treaty to Limit
ABMs and an (interim) Agreement on Offensive Missiles.

The agreements gave substance to the Administration's claim that
"détente"—an era of peaceful coexistence and cooperation—was more than
a pious hope.

"Turn Up The Cloud Machine, Angels Enter From The Left—"

Don Wright. *The Miami News,* 1972.

The Vietnam peace agreement of 1973 paved the way for a further
relaxation of tensions. Veteran cold warriors had trouble adjusting to the
new spirit of cordiality.

The Odd Couple

Bill Mauldin. *The Sun-Times* (Chicago), 1973.
Copyright 1973—Chicago Sun-Times. Reproduced by courtesy of
Wil-Jo Associates, Inc., and Bill Mauldin.

Some of the Kremlin leaders reportedly were cool to détente, but Brezhnev quickly proved to them that it had some practical applications. Faced with an embarrassing shortage of wheat in 1972, the Russians went shopping in the American market and came home with a bargain.

By mid-1974 Soviet-American détente appeared to be one of the major accomplishments of the Nixon Administration.

"Détente"

Drawing by Richter; © 1974 The New Yorker Magazine, Inc.

16

Ping-Pong and Pig Bristles

Another major foreign-policy breakthrough of the Nixon Administration was the opening to the East. Ever since Chiang Kai-shek's Republic of China had retreated to Taiwan, his was the only Chinese government the United States recognized. As far as Washington was concerned, the Peking government didn't officially exist.

Year after year, the question of Chinese representation came up in the United Nations. Without fail the United States opposed any change, and Taiwan continued to fill China's seat. In the meantime, the United Nations' membership roster more than doubled.

"Do they discriminate against size?"

Guernsey LePelley. *The Christian Science Monitor*, 1969.

The Nationalist government had few more loyal supporters than Nixon. The President's anti-Communist, anti-Peking credentials were impeccable. And he therefore could do what no Democratic President, whose party was tarred with the stigma of "losing" China, had dared to do—reach an accommodation with Red China.

The first sign of a change in relations between the two countries was China's invitation to an American ping-pong team in April, 1971.

High Lob

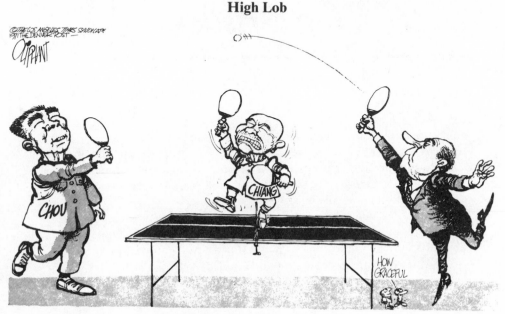

Pat Oliphant. *The Denver Post*, 1971.

In July presidential adviser Henry Kissinger secretly flew to the People's Republic to test the water. The temperature was fine, and he set the stage for the President's visit in 1972.

A major hurdle blocked the President's path to Peking: the issue of China's admission to the United Nations. That posed a dilemma. If Washington voted for mainland China's admission on Peking's terms, it would have to abandon an old ally, the Nationalist government on Taiwan.

Ranan Lurie, 1971.

The Administration's solution was a "two-China" proposal: admit mainland China but let Taiwan keep its seat. But since both "Chinas" claimed to represent all the Chinese people, the U. S. solution pleased neither one.

"Three to tango, three to tango . . ."

Don Wright. *The Miami News*, 1971.

At the end of October '71 the General Assembly voted overwhelmingly to admit Communist China and expel the Nationalists.

Tony Auth. *The Philadelphia Inquirer*, 1971.

The President made his historic visit to China in February '72. It was an election year, and some Democrats questioned Nixon's motives.

Marco Polo

Ray Osrin. *The Plain Dealer* (Cleveland), 1972.

Conservatives in the President's own party also had misgivings about his trip.

**"I suppose you're going to tell me
you were out building bridges again. . . ."**

Don Wright. *The Miami News*, 1972.

But the majority of Nixon's fellow Americans seemed to share his delight in getting a glimpse of what was going on behind the bamboo curtain.

The main thrust of the Sino-American talks concerned opportunities for trade and educational, scientific and cultural exchanges between the two countries. A sudden spurt in two-way trade seemed unlikely.

"I am suddenly aware of the reason for our 20-year lack of interest."

Pat Oliphant. *The Denver Post*, 1971.

Far more important than trade in the long run was the fact that the Administration had succeeded in opening a dialogue. And that dialogue was bound to affect future relations between the world's great powers.

"I'm not sure of the rules, but it looks like an interesting game."

Hugh Haynie. *The Courier-Journal* (Louisville, Kentucky), 1971.

17

The Mideast Quagmire

Tom Darcy. *Newsday* (Garden City, New York), 1974.

When the Nixon Administration took office, it had one overriding objective in the Middle East: achieve a peace settlement between Israel and its Arab neighbors and, in the process, maintain an evenhanded policy. It didn't take long for the experts to discover that "evenhanded" doesn't translate. In Arabic it means "pro-Israeli" and in Hebrew, "pro-Arab."

Israelis felt Washington was helping the Arabs by holding out on vital military aid. They noted that Egypt's allies, by contrast—the Russians and, on a smaller scale, the French—were supplying Egypt with almost an entire new army and air force.

Arms for the Love of Allah

Gene Basset, 1970.

Parts of the peace package that Secretary Rogers brought with him to the Middle East also upset Israelis. The United States insisted that Israel, with the exception of some "insubstantial alterations," return to the vulnerable pre-June, 1967, boundaries.

"Jump off and you'll get a lifetime supply of shark repellent."

Bill Mauldin. *The Sun-Times* (Chicago), 1971.
Copyright 1971—Chicago Sun Times. Reproduced by courtesy of
Wil-Jo Associates, Inc., and Bill Mauldin.

The Egyptians were also unhappy with the United States. Although they had broken off relations with Washington in 1967, they had agreed to receive Secretary Rogers in 1970. (It was the first visit by a U. S. Secretary of State since John Foster Dulles's trip in 1953.) They had indicated to Rogers their willingness to make major concessions to Israel, but Rogers, they complained, had failed to exact any reciprocal concessions from the Israelis.

The one concrete achievement of the Rogers peace missions was the August, 1970, cease-fire agreement between Israel and Egypt. But that was small comfort in Foggy Bottom. There was grave apprehension in the State Department over the continued expansion of Soviet arms and influence in the Middle East.

" 'Scuse Please—New Delivery!"

Pat Oliphant. *The Denver Post*, 1971.

When Golda Meir arrived in Washington in December, 1971, to renew her plea for more Phantom fighter-bombers, the Administration was unexpectedly receptive. President Nixon promised to sell Israel Phantoms and Skyhawks; they would be delivered over the next two to three years.

Ranan Lurie, 1971.

The arms deal with Israel did not sit well with the Egyptians. But President Sadat, instead of leaning all the harder on the Russians, abruptly asked the thousands of Soviet military advisers stationed in his country to leave.

Tony Auth. *The Philadelphia Inquirer,* 1972.

Sadat had predicted that 1972 would be Egypt's "year of decision." That threatened confrontation took place a year later. On October 6, 1973, on Yom Kippur, the holiest day of the Jewish calendar, Egyptian and Syrian troops attacked Israel. The war shattered two myths: that Israel was invincible, and that the Arab forces couldn't master modern military technology.

The United States took a hand in ending the war. It also played a role in trying to cement the peace. Kissinger, who had taken over the portfolio of Secretary of State in August, 1973, in addition to his duties as the President's principal national security adviser, shuttled back and forth from capital to capital in hopes of securing peace terms acceptable to all sides.

"There Goes the 8:05"

Don Wright. *The Miami News,* 1974.

At the end of his third tour in as many months, Kissinger announced on January 17, 1974, the signing of an Egyptian-Israeli disengagement agreement. It was a personal as well as a diplomatic triumph.

Kissinger tried to work his magic again in early 1975, but this time the spell was broken. Both sides blamed the other's intransigence. The shuttle crash-landed. And peace in the Middle East remained a mirage.

"Peace . . ."

Tony Auth. *The Philadelphia Inquirer,* 1975.

173

18

Crisis in Leadership

President Nixon's historic visit to China and his successful Moscow summit meeting in May '72 gave him momentary relief from the war with his critics at home. That domestic war reached a new level of intensity a year later. In the spring of '73, after the Paris cease-fire agreement was signed, the President ordered the bombing of Cambodia. That decision sparked a full-blown constitutional crisis. The President claimed that as Commander-in-Chief he had the authority to bomb. Congress disagreed and claimed that only Congress had the power to commit the country to war.

James J. Dobbins. *Boston Herald-American*, 1973.

The tug-of-war between the Chief Executive and Congress is as American as apple pie. Between the two world wars, it was Congress that frequently stepped on the President's toes when it came to foreign-policy decisions. After 1939 the roles were reversed. Republican and Democratic Presidents alike enlarged their powers at the expense of Congress, sometimes with its consent.

In Nixon's case, Congress felt the President had gone too far. His authority to make war wasn't the only issue. Many congressmen were alarmed by what they considered the President's high-handed use of executive privilege. Nixon aides claimed at one point that executive privilege gave members of the White House staff blanket immunity from testifying. That prompted Senator Fulbright's rejoinder that "the power to withhold testimony is the power to strangle Congress." The President had also claimed executive privilege in refusing to release the tape recordings of his White House conversations.

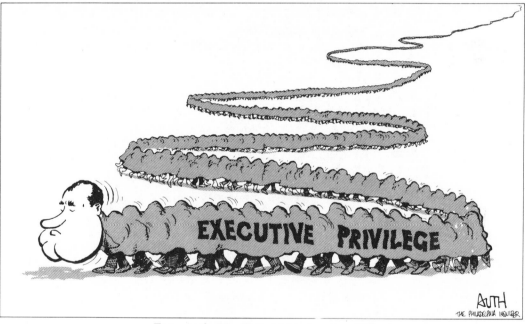

Tony Auth. *The Philadelphia Inquirer,* 1973.

The President insisted that the real problem lay not with the executive branch but with the legislative. The President hadn't usurped powers: Congress had abdicated them. If there was a constitutional crisis, the remedy lay with Congress. It should put its house in order.

"Man, If You Want To Stay In This Game, You'd Better Get In Shape."

Herbert L. Block. *The Washington Post,* 1973.
Copyright 1973 by Herblock in The Washington Post

Try as he might, Nixon was unable to exorcise the Watergate monster. In 1973, as the investigations got closer and closer to the Oval Office, it became perfectly clear that the President's preoccupation with Watergate might impair his effectiveness as the country's chief foreign-policy maker.

"Poor Fellow—First He Called Me Mr. Pompigate and Then Mr. Waterdou"

John Fischetti. *Chicago Daily News,* 1973.

By 1974 Henry Kissinger, in his dual capacity as Secretary of State and the President's national security adviser, was carrying a large part of the foreign-policy burden.

Tony Auth. *The Philadelphia Inquirer,* 1974.

In June *Newsweek* wrote a cover story on Super K. Many Americans felt the peripatetic diplomat well deserved the title. Even critics had grudging admiration for Kissinger's indefatigable efforts to bind the world's wounds.

Don Wright, *The Miami News*, 1974.

The Wonderful World of Henry Kissinger

Paul Szep. *The Boston Globe*, 1975.

But Kissinger wasn't a substitute for the nation's chief executive. By mid-'74 the President was more and more deeply ensnared in the spreading scandal of Watergate. The crisis in leadership in Washington came at a time when Europe was also in the throes of political turmoil. In May, West Germany's Willy Brandt was forced to resign, following the revelation that a close aide was an East German spy. In Britain, voters went to the polls twice in one year, first to put Harold Wilson back into 10 Downing Street, the next time to keep him there.

"What do they mean, 'crisis in leadership'?"

Bill Mauldin. *The Sun-Times* (Chicago), 1974.
Copyright 1974—Chicago Sun Times. Reproduced by courtesy of
Wil-Jo Associates, Inc., and Bill Mauldin.

On August 9, 1974, Nixon became the first American President to resign the office. Since his appointed successor, House Republican Leader Ford, had spent most of his political life on the Hill, observers predicted a long honeymoon between the White House and Congress. But the honeymoon quickly soured. Congressional critics were angry with the President for trying to pin the blame for his foreign-policy problems on Congress:

"It's A Variation Of An Old Game—Now Hold Still."

Herbert L. Block. *The Washington Post*, 1975.
Copyright 1975 by Herblock in The Washington Post

The President was equally unhappy with the Democratically controlled Congress for failing to cooperate with him. By 1975 a new debate between the powers of the Executive and the powers of Congress was in the making.

"Sometimes we mule skinners have to give a little ground"

David Simpson. *Tulsa Tribune*, 1975.

19

Interdependence: Like It or Leave It

While the President and his Secretary of State grappled with Congress over control of U. S. foreign policy, the international community was struggling with a long agenda of problems requiring global solutions. Near the top of the list was the world economic crisis. The crisis meant different things to different people. For the industrialized, oil-importing nations, which suddenly found themselves paying four times as much for petroleum after the 1973 Mideast war as they had before the war, the crisis was a three-letter word, O-I-L.

Neal von Hedemann, 1974.

"You're like a bunch of . . . of . . . of . . . CAPITALISTS!"

Dennis Renault. *Sacramento Bee* (California), 1974.

As Americans turned down their thermostats and reduced their speed (and highway fatalities), the members of the Organization of Petroleum Exporting Countries savored their new economic weapon.

"One thing I've found out about oil . . . it's intoxicating."

Pat Oliphant. *The Denver Post*, 1973.

The United States and the other major oil consumers considered the possibility of counter-cartels.

Wizard of Id

Brant Parker, 1975.

A major concern in Washington was the prospect of billions of petrodollars accumulating in Mideast coffers while industrialized nations' economies stagnated. By 1975, however, some of the petrodollars were finding their way back into circulation.

In addition to investments, petrodollars financed arms orders and nuclear reactors. Some were even used to hire Vietnam veterans to train Saudi Arabia's palace guard.

Michael J. Lane. *Evening Sun* (Baltimore), 1975.

"And as a last resort in hand-to-hand combat, you can always strike the enemy with your wallet."

Ralph Dunagin. *Sentinel-Star* (Orlando, Florida), 1975.

While the industrialized nations fought inflation and recession and complained about the high price of crude, the developing countries made it clear that their sympathies were with the oil exporters. For years, they claimed, the industrialized countries had been buying commodities from the Third World at bargain prices and making a handsome profit on manufactured exports. The rising cost of the developing countries' imports more than offset the help they received in the form of trade concessions or aid.

Foreign aid had been a controversial subject ever since the Marshall Plan. Over the years it had been a favorite target of congressional budget parers.

Open Season

Burges Green. *The Providence Journal,* 1966.

"Now that dollars are worth less, we'll need more of them."

Bill Mauldin. *The Sun-Times* (Chicago), 1971.
Copyright 1971—Chicago Sun-Times. Reproduced by courtesy of
Wil-Jo Associates, Inc., and Bill Mauldin.

Some Americans, even though they supported foreign aid in principle, felt too much of it ended up in the wrong pockets.

The opponents of the foreign-assistance program didn't kill it but they succeeded in keeping the level well below Administration requests.

The problems of economic development, despite a First and then a Second United Nations Development Decade, wouldn't go away. If anything, they appeared to be getting worse.

The world's population reached 4 billion in 1975 and threatened to grow by another 2.5 billion by the end of the century. Would the world be able to increase food output enough to keep up with the population?

Al Liederman. *Long Island Press* (New York), 1974.

Growth became a major issue in the '70s. Some futurists warned that if present growth trends continued, the world would run out of food, energy, and other resources within one hundred years. The industrialized nations tended to put the blame on the developing countries and their high population-growth rates. The developing nations claimed it was the rich, not the poor, who were exhausting the earth's resources. The United States alone consumes about 40 percent of the world's output of raw materials (not including food).

The issue was joined at the 1972 UN Conference on the Human Environment in Stockholm. While some rich nations called for pollution controls, many poor nations wished out loud that they had enough industry to create a pollution problem. All agreed that, in the end, threats to the environment, regardless of their source, affect rich and poor alike.

Pogo

Walt Kelly, 1970.

"I Knew There'd Be a Catch in It When They Said the Meek Would Inherit the Earth"

John Fischetti. *Chicago Daily News,* 1972.

Following Stockholm, the UN convened world conferences on food, on population, on the law of the sea. The one theme common to all was the growing interdependence of man on "spaceship earth."

While few Americans challenged the principle of interdependence, many questioned whether the United Nations and its specialized agencies were the right forum for curing global problems.

From the outset, a very small but vocal minority in this country viewed the United Nations as a haven for undesirables.

Trojan Horse

Joseph Parrish. *The Tribune* (Chicago), 1949.

Most Americans, however, subscribed to the view that if the United Nations didn't exist, it would have to be invented.

The Small Society

Brickman. *The Evening Star* (Washington, D.C.), 1966.

The machinery for keeping the peace was all there, spelled out in the Charter. It was up to the members to make it work.

"Oh, It'll Work—Just a Matter of Getting It Started!"

Bil Canfield. *Star-Ledger* (Newark), 1970.

Even UN partisans, however, were dissatisfied with the United Nations' lack of progress in such critical areas as disarmament and controlling the spread of nuclear weapons. The two major nuclear powers were all for keeping the weapons out of the hands of the have-nots.

"—If we only had some kind of a pill."

John Fawcett, *The Providence Journal*, 1966.

Many of the nuclear have-nots, on the other hand, were anxious to join the exclusive nuclear club as soon as they could afford the dues.

B. C.

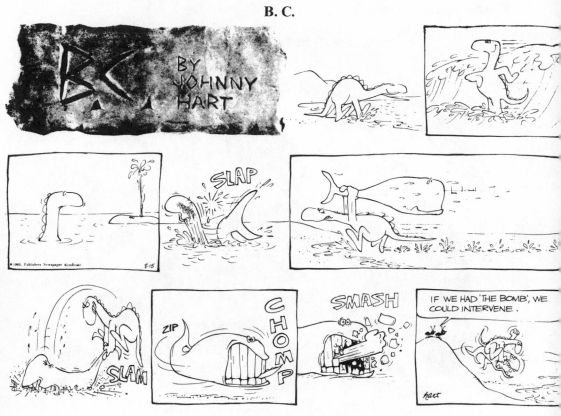

John Hart, 1965.

Much of the current disenchantment with the United Nations stems from the shift in the balance of power. When the UN Charter was signed at San Francisco in 1945, the United States, with the help of Latin America, controlled a sizable block of votes in the General Assembly. The United States today no longer has that kind of control. It can't count on the other 137 members to dance to its tune. Increasingly, it finds itself outshouted and outvoted, a victim of the "tyranny" of the new UN majority.

United Nations

Tony Auth. *The Philadelphia Inquirer*, 1971.

As it celebrated its Bicentennial, the United States was the richest and most powerful nation on earth. But it had learned the hard way that its power, great as it was, was not unlimited.

"Of course I'm in charge—I think."

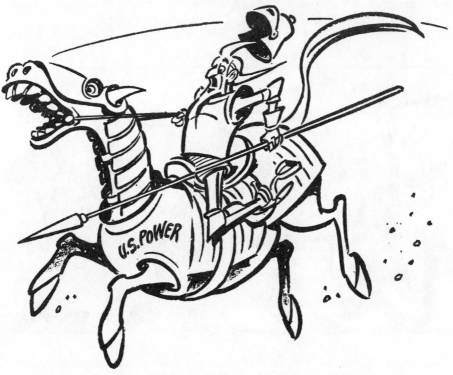

Robert Bastian. *San Francisco Chronicle,* 1966.

Guide to Cartoon Sources

1

197

16 James Akin, A general arguing of the Maine question. 1832. Library Company of Philadelphia.

17 David Claypoole Johnston, Symptoms of a Locked Jaw. c. 1834. Courtesy of The New-York Historical Society, New York City.

18 James Akin, A "Hickory" Apology. 1836. Courtesy of The New-York Historical Society, New York City.

19 The Old Lion and the Cock what won't fight. Anon. 1836. Courtesy of The New-York Historical Society, New York City.

20 Edward Williams Clay, Uncle Sam's Taylorifics. 1846. Courtesy of The New-York Historical Society, New York City.

21 G. Thomas, The Mexican Commander. Lithographed by Sarony & Major. 1846. Courtesy of The New-York Historical Society, New York City.

21 Plucked. Anon. From *Yankee Doodle,* 1847. Science and Technology Research Center, The New York Public Library, Astor, Lenox, and Tilden foundations.

22 Defence of the California Bank. Anon. 1849. Courtesy of The New-York Historical Society, New York City.

23 Soloque, Emperor of Hayti, creating a Grand Duke. Anon. c. 1856. Reproduced from the collection of the Library of Congress.

25 Louis Maurer, A Serviceable Garment. 1856. Courtesy of The New-York Historical Society, New York City.

3

26 Currier & Ives, John Bull Makes A Discovery. c. 1861. Prints Division, The New York Public Library, Astor, Lenox, and Tilden foundations.

28 *Harper's Weekly,* November 30, 1861. Reproduced from the collection of the Library of Congress.

29 Anthony Hochstein, Our Foreign Relations. 1864. Prints Division, The New York Public Library, Astor, Lenox, and Tilden foundations.

30 William Newman, Reconstruction—the old Map mended. From *Frank Leslie's Budget of Fun,* 1865. Reprinted from William Murrell, *A History of American Graphic Humor.* 1967. Courtesy of Cooper Square Publishers, Inc., New York City.

31 Our New Senators. Anon. 1867. The Granger Collection.

32 Thomas Nast, The Apple of Discord. *Harper's Weekly,* October 5, 1872. Prints Division, The New York Public Library, Astor, Lenox, and Tilden foundations.

33 "G.," Shipwrecked Patriotism. *Puck,* February 22, 1882. General Research and Humanities Division, The New York Public Library, Astor, Lenox, and Tilden foundations.

34 Joseph Keppler, The Opening of the Congressional Session. *Puck,* December 7, 1887. Prints Division, The New York Public Library, Astor, Lenox, and Tilden foundations.

35 Bernard Gillam, The Goose That Lays the Golden Eggs. *Judge,* September 8, 1888. Reproduced from the collection of the Library of Congress.

36 Joseph Keppler, At Last! *Puck,* January 18, 1888. Prints Division, The New York Public Library, Astor, Lenox, and Tilden foundations.

4

38 J. S. Pughe, She Is Getting Too Feeble to Hold Them. *Puck,* November 18, 1896. Reproduced from the collection of the Library of Congress.

39 Joseph Keppler, Consistency. *Puck,* January 21, 1891. Prints Division, The New York Public Library, Astor, Lenox, and Tilden foundations.

39 Charles Nelan, "The Boy Stood on the Burning Deck." From Charles Nelan, *Cartoons of Our War With Spain.* New York, F. A. Stokes, 1898. American History Division, The New York Public Library, Astor, Lenox, and Tilden foundations.

40 Charles L. Bartholomew, Make Him Walk Spanish. *Minneapolis Journal,* July 12, 1898. From *Cartoons of the Spanish War by Bart.* Minneapolis, Minnesota, The Journal Printing Co., 1899. American History Division, The New York Public Library, Astor, Lenox, and Tilden foundations.

41 Grant Hamilton, The Spanish Brute. *Judge,* July 9, 1898. Reproduced from the collection of the Library of Congress.

41 J. Campbell Cory, The Cares of a Growing Family. *The Bee,* May 25, 1898. General Research and Humanities Division, The New York Public Library, Astor, Lenox, and Tilden foundations.

42 William H. Walker, Our Expansive Uncle, But It's Only Temporary. *Life,* December 28, 1899. © Old *Life* Magazine. Reproduced from the collection of the Library of Congress.

5

44 Albert Levering, A Story of the China Shop. *Harper's Weekly*, March 5, 1904. General Research and Humanities Division, The New York Public Library, Astor, Lenox, and Tilden foundations.

46 Crane, "The man behind the egg." *The New York Times* Magazine Supplement, November 15, 1903. © 1903 by The New York Times Company. Reprinted by permission.

47 Louis Dalrymple, The World's Constable. *Judge*, January 7, 1905. The Granger Collection.

48 Oscar Edward Cesare, Out of the Depths. 1915. From *One Hundred Cartoons by Cesare.* Boston, Small, Maynard, 1916. Prints Division, The New York Public Library, Astor, Lenox, and Tilden foundations.

49 Jay N. Darling, The Python. c. 1917. From *Ding's Half Century*, John M. Henry, ed. New York, Duell, Sloan & Pearce, 1962. J. N. ("Ding") Darling Foundation, Fleming Building, Des Moines, Iowa.

50 Robert Minor, Army Medical Examiner. *The Masses*, August, 1916. Reprinted from Murrell, *op. cit.* Courtesy of Cooper Square Publishers, Inc., New York City.

51   Jay N. Darling, How We Forced Germany Into the War. c. 1917. From *Ding's Half Century*, *op.cit.* J. N. ("Ding") Darling Foundation, Fleming Building, Des Moines, Iowa.

52   J. H. Donahey, Nothing Left but the Howl. c. 1919. From *The War In Cartoons,* George Joseph Hecht, ed. New York, E. P. Dutton, 1919. © *The Plain Dealer* (Cleveland).

6

54   John T. McCutcheon, Interrupting the Ceremony. *The Tribune* (Chicago), December 25, 1918. Reprinted by permission of the Chicago Tribune-New York News Syndicate, Inc. All Rights Reserved.

55   Jay N. Darling, The Prescription That Went Astray. c. 1919. From Jay N. Darling, *Books of Cartoons*, Vol. 4. Des Moines, Des Moines Register, 1920. J. N. ("Ding") Darling Foundation, Fleming Building, Des Moines, Iowa.

56   J. H. Donahey, Getting a Taste of It. c. 1919. © *The Plain Dealer* (Cleveland).

57   Jay N. Darling, The League of Nations Argument in a Nutshell. c. 1919. From *Ding's Half Century*, *op.cit.* J. N. ("Ding") Darling Foundation, Fleming Building, Des Moines, Iowa.

58   Boardman Robinson, Signed. June, 1919. Collection unknown. Reprinted from Murrell, *op. cit.* Courtesy of Cooper Square Publishers, Inc., New York City.

59   Jay N. Darling, The One Animal That Wouldn't Go Into the Ark. c. 1920. From Jay N. Darling, *Books of Cartoons*, Vol. 4. *op.cit.* J. N. ("Ding") Darling Foundation, Fleming Building, Des Moines, Iowa.

60   Rollin Kirby, Triumphal Entry Into Normalcy. April 14, 1921. From Rollin Kirby, *Highlights: A Cartoon History of the Nineteen Twenties*. New York, W. F. Payson, 1931.

61   John T. McCutcheon. *The Tribune* (Chicago), April 7, 1920. Reprintd by permission of the Chicago Tribune-New York News Syndicate, Inc. All Rights Reserved.

62   Jay N. Darling, "We Told You It Wouldn't Work!" c. 1920. From *Ding's Half Century, op.cit.* J. N. ("Ding") Darling Foundation, Fleming Building, Des Moines, Iowa.

63   Nelson Harding, Our Greatest Naval Victory. *The Brooklyn Daily Eagle,* February 3, 1922.

63   Carey Orr, The Roots. *The Tribune* (Chicago), c. 1921. Reprinted by permission of the Chicago Tribune-New York News Syndicate, Inc. All Rights Reserved.

64   Homer Stinson, "It looks fine, but I can't make it breathe!" *Dayton Daily News*, c. 1922.

65   Jay N. Darling, The Round Trip to the Disarmament Conference. 1926. From *Ding's Half Century, op.cit.* J. N. ("Ding") Darling Foundation, Fleming Building, Des Moines, Iowa.

66   William A. Ireland, Married Again. *The Columbus Dispatch,* August 28, 1928.

67   Carey Orr, Another Blindfold Test. *The Tribune* (Chicago), 1928. Reprinted by permission of the Chicago Tribune-New York News Syndicate, Inc. All Rights Reserved.

7

68 Oscar Edward Cesare, The Open Door. *Outlook,* October 30, 1931.

69 Hugh Hutton, The Sleeping Giant Begins to Feel It. *The Philadelphia Inquirer,* July 18, 1937.

70 William Gropper, Another Pact. 1936. Courtesy of the ACA Galleries, Inc., New York City.

71 Fred Ellis, Labor's Day in Nuremberg. *The Daily Worker,* September 11, 1937. Courtesy of Mrs. Fred Ellis.

72 Vaughn Shoemaker, Too Hungry to Complain. *Chicago Daily News,* 1938.

73 Grover Page, Consultation. *The Courier-Journal* (Louisville), September 30, 1938.

74 Fred O. Seibel, Sticking His Neck Out. *Richmond Times-Dispatch,* May 2, 1939.

75 David Low, Rendezvous. 1939. Cartoon by David Low by arrangement with the Trustees and the *London Evening Standard.*

8

76 C. D. Batchelor, "Come on in. I'll treat you right. I used to know your Daddy." *Daily News* (New York), April 25, 1936.© New York News Inc.

77 Carey Orr, The Only Way We Can Save Her. *The Tribune* (Chicago), September 9, 1939. Reprinted by permission of the Chicago Tribune-New York News Syndicate, Inc. All Rights Reserved.

78 Albert Hirschfeld, The Isolationist. *New Masses,* June 21, 1938.

79 Daniel Robert Fitzpatrick, Most Popular Baby of the Campaign. *St. Louis Post-Dispatch,* October 26, 1940.

80 Daniel Robert Fitzpatrick, The People Try to Get the White House Viewpoint. *St. Louis Post-Dispatch,* February 6, 1941.

81 Lute Pease, Any More? *Newark News,* 1942. Reprinted by permission of Richmond Newspapers Inc.

82 Bill Crawford, V for Victory. *Newark News,* 1945. Reprinted by permission of Newspaper Enterprise Association (or NEA).

83 M. Bernstein. *PM,* August 15, 1945.

9

84 Jay N. Darling, Eventually, Why Not Now? 1945. From *Ding's Half Century, op.cit.* J. N. ("Ding") Darling Foundation, Fleming Building, Des Moines, Iowa.

85 Jay N. Darling, And Company Already Arriving. c. 1945. From *Ding's Half Century, op.cit.* J. N. ("Ding") Darling Foundation, Fleming Building, Des Moines, Iowa.

86 Charles G. Werner, But What Part Shall the Meek Inherit? *The Indianapolis Star,* July 5, 1949.

87 Jay N. Darling, A Caller from Across the Sea. c. 1946. From *Ding's Half Century, op.cit.* J. N. ("Ding") Darling Foundation, Fleming Building, Des Moines, Iowa.

88 Burt R. Thomas, Nobody Is Happy. *The Detroit News,* 1949.

89 Edwin Marcus, Great Expectations. *The New York Times,*
    1947. © 1947 by The New York Times Company. Reprinted by permission.

90 Roy Justus, Step on it, Doc! *The Minneapolis Star,* 1947.

91 Joseph Parrish, Some Day They'll Come Crawling Back to Her. *The Tribune*
    (Chicago), June 29, 1949. Reprinted by permission of the Chicago
    Tribune-New York News Syndicate, Inc. All Rights Reserved.

92 Richard Q. Yardley, Unintentional Cupid. *The Sun* (Baltimore), July, 1949.

93 Dan Dowling, An Increasingly Difficult Neighborhood. *New York Herald
    Tribune,* May 28, 1950. Dan Dowling editorial cartoon. Courtesy of Field
    Newspaper Syndicate.

10

94 M. Bernstein, Prisoner of War. *PM,* November 6, 1945.

95 Paule Loring, How Long? *The Evening Bulletin* (Providence), January 29,
    1949.

96 Burt R. Thomas, Hard to Recognize. *The Detroit News,* November 27, 1949.

97 Edwin Marcus, Starting Something? *The New York Times,* 1950. © 1950 by
    The New York Times Company. Reprinted by permission.

98 Reg Manning, Hemmed In. April 16, 1951. Reg Manning, McNaught
    Syndicate, Inc.

99 Bill Mauldin, "And the best part is that *he's* paying *us* for the ride."
    September 12, 1958. Copyright 1958—St. Louis Post-Dispatch. Reproduced
    by courtesy of Bill Mauldin.

100 Richard Q. Yardley, "Let's You and Him Fight." *The Sun* (Baltimore),
    c. 1958.

101 John R. Stampone, Demonstration on Filling a Vacuum. *The Army Times,*
    December 14, 1956.

102 Herbert L. Block, "Well, It's Sort Of New With Us." *The Washington Post,*
    January 8, 1957. From *Herblock's Special For Today* (Simon & Schuster,
    1958).

103 Ed Valtman, Not As Impossible As It May Seem. *The Hartford Times,* 1956.

104 Hy Rosen, Mideast Tableau. *Times-Union,* May 15, 1958. Rosen—Albany,
    N. Y., Times-Union.

105 Warren King, Cleopatra. *Daily News* (New York), July 3, 1959.

11

106 John Milt Morris, But How About the Basic Design! AP Newsfeatures, 1953.
    © The Associated Press.

107 Scott Long, The Cheshire Cat. *The Minneapolis Tribune,* October 2, 1955.

108 Herbert L. Block. *The Washington Post,* 1959. From *Straight Herblock*
    (Simon & Schuster, 1964).

109 Bill Mauldin. October 14, 1960. Copyright 1960—St. Louis Post-Dispatch. Reproduced by courtesy of Bill Mauldin.

110 Bill Mauldin, ". . . And there's a bad crevasse just past this ridge . . ." May 17, 1961. Copyright 1961—St. Louis Post-Dispatch. Reproduced by courtesy of Bill Mauldin.

111 Hank Barrow, "Now This Is the Gissile Map, I Mean Gappile Miss, I Mean . . ." *The Omaha World-Herald,* February 10, 1961.

112 Charles G. Werner, "Kennedy back trouble is big capitalist lie. . . ." *The Indianapolis Star,* June 25, 1961.

113 Don Wright, "See how many are staying on our side." *The Miami News,* 1961.

114 Richard Q. Yardley, A Doctrine Discuss'd. *The Sun* (Baltimore), October 17, 1962.

115 Warren King, Showdown. *Daily News* (New York), October 21, 1962.

116 Richard Q. Yardley, "I'd Reconsider If I Were You!" *The Sun* (Baltimore), October 23, 1962.

117 Hy Rosen, Retreat. *The Times-Union,* October 30, 1962. Rosen—Albany, N. Y., Times-Union.

12

118 Ed Holland, The Girl He Left Behind. 1960. Reprinted courtesy of the Chicago Tribune.

119 Burges Green, ". . . And you, what would you like for Christmas?" *The Providence Journal,* December 18, 1963. Providence Journal Co.

120 Guernsey LePelley, "Stop Enjoying Yourself." August 12, 1964. LePelley in *The Christian Science Monitor* © 1964 TCSPS.

120 John Fischetti, "Forward!" April 20, 1964. Publishers Newspaper Syndicate.

121 Paul Conrad, ". . . Drunk? . . . Of course I'm not drunk!!" © 1965 Los Angeles Times.

122 Clifford K. Berryman. *Washington Star,* July 8, 1944.

123 Pierre Bellocq, "I'm here, Ludwig . . . Have no fear!" *The Philadelphia Inquirer,* February 20, 1964.

124 Gene Basset, "How much ist das bombie in das vindow?" Scripps-Howard Newspaper Alliance, c. 1965.

125 Hugh Haynie, "If you won't play my way I'll take my ball and go home." *The Courier-Journal* (Louisville), 1965.

126 Richard Q. Yardley, The Adamant Concierge. *The Sun* (Baltimore), 1966.

13

127 Ray Osrin, "It's Not THAT Common!" *The Plain Dealer* (Cleveland), May 14, 1967.

128 Robert Bastian, "Before we take you into our club the Membership Committee has a few questions." May 18, 1967. Reprinted by permission of the *San Francisco Chronicle*.

129 Pierre Bellocq, "Forget It, Messieurs, Nothing Can Be Done." *The Philadelphia Inquirer*, March 27, 1968.

130 C. Sanford Huffaker, "Doc, my heart's fine, but I keep getting this pain in my wallet . . ." *The News and Observer* (Raleigh, North Carolina), 1971. Rothco Cartoons.

131 Don Wright, "More Gum, Connally—And Get a Longer Stick." *The Miami News*, October 25, 1971.

132 Pat Oliphant, "Take It Off! Take It All Off!!" September 29, 1971. Editorial cartoon by Pat Oliphant. Copyright Washington Star. Reprinted with permission Los Angeles Times Syndicate.

133 Gib Crockett, "And to think I set him up in business!" *Washington Star*, August 1, 1971.

133 Ray Osrin. *The Plain Dealer* (Cleveland), December 6, 1969.

134 Robert Graysmith, "I'll carry the bar . . ." *San Francisco Chronicle*, June 2, 1971. © Chronicle Publishing Co., 1971.

135 Herbert L. Block, "It's From Europe. They're Thinking About Having A 'Year of the United States.' " March 20, 1974. Copyright 1974 by Herblock in The Washington Post.

14

136 Pierre Bellocq, "We've got to operate, and fast!" *The Philadelphia Inquirer*, July 30, 1965.

137 Frank Interlandi, "The pattern as a whole is undecipherable . . ." *The Los Angeles Times*, February 21, 1965.

138 Bill Mauldin, "Dr. Lippmann wants to amputate, but Dr. Alsop says to take more shots." August 20, 1965. Copyright 1965—Chicago Sun-Times. Reproduced by courtesy of Wil-Jo Associates, Inc., and Bill Mauldin.

139 Isadore J. Parker, "Not an effective gas? . . . It caused nausea and tears as far away as the State Department." © 1965 Washington Post Company.

140 Pat Oliphant, "Could you point out the ground you've taken? . . ." February 16, 1966. Editorial cartoon by Pat Oliphant. Copyright Washington Star. Reprinted with permission Los Angeles Times Syndicate.

141 Bill Mauldin, The Strategists. February 16, 1966. Copyright 1966—Chicago Sun-Times. Reproduced by courtesy of Wil-Jo Associates, Inc., and Bill Mauldin.

142 David Levine. *The New York Review of Books*, 1966. Reprinted with permission from *The New York Review of Books*. © 1966 The New York Review.

143 Bil Canfield, "Only Thing We're Sure Of—There Is a Tonkin Gulf!" *Star-Ledger* (Newark), February 27, 1968.

144 Cal Alley, Middle Course. *The Commercial Appeal* (Memphis, Tennessee), February 28, 1968.

145 Wayne Stayskal, "Happy birthday to youuuu . . . Happy birthday to . . ." *Chicago Today*, 1969. By permission of Wayne Stayskal for Chicago Tribune.

145 John Fischetti, "I never did say how, but I told you I'd get you out of Vietnam." *Chicago Daily News*, May 16, 1970.

146 Bill Mauldin, "No, Hanson, You Didn't Find a Box of Bullets and Two Bags of Rice. You Captured an Ammo Dump and a Supply Depot." May 13, 1970. Copyright 1970—Chicago Sun-Times. Reproduced by courtesy of Wil-Jo Associates, Inc., and Bill Mauldin.

147 Paul Conrad, It became necessary to destroy (a) South Vietnam, (b) Laos, (c) Cambodia, (d) Thailand, (e) all of the above—to save Southeast Asia. July 1, 1970. © 1970 Los Angeles Times.

148 Pat Oliphant, "Come on out, Richard—We know you're in there!" June 8, 1971. Editorial cartoon by Pat Oliphant. Copyright Washington Star. Reprinted with permission Los Angeles Times Syndicate.

148 Garry B. Trudeau, "Doonesbury." March 8, 1972. Copyright, 1975, G. B. Trudeau/distributed by Universal Press Syndicate.

149 Corky Trinidad, Snow White and the Seven Experiments. *Honolulu Star-Bulletin*, June 1, 1970. Los Angeles Times Syndicate.

150 Pat Oliphant, "Anyone care to give again to Vietnam . . . ?" January 19, 1975. Editorial cartoon by Pat Oliphant. Copyright Washington Star. Reprinted with permission Los Angeles Times Syndicate.

150 Paul Szep. *The Boston Globe*, March 8, 1975.

151 James J. Dobbins, End of the Domino Theory. *Boston Herald-American*, April 3, 1975.

15

153 Bil Canfield, "You Against Protection or Something?" *Star-Ledger* (Newark), April 11, 1969.

154 Herbert L. Block, "As Soon As Mirv Is Ready He'll Go To The Conference With You." Copyright 1969 by Herblock in The Washington Post.

155 Robert Graysmith, "Gentlemen, the main course is getting hot!" *San Francisco Chronicle,* December 10, 1969. © Chronicle Publishing Co., 1969.

156 Pat Oliphant, "Do Me A Favor—Help Me Drop It!" August 18, 1970. Editorial cartoon by Pat Oliphant. Copyright Washington Star. Reprinted with permission Los Angeles Times Syndicate.

157 Ranan Lurie. December 30, 1970. Lurie, Newsweek International. Syndicated nationally by the Los Angeles Times, internationally by The New York Times.

158 Don Wright, "Turn Up The Cloud Machine, Angels Enter From The Left—" *The Miami News*, 1972.

159 Bill Mauldin, The Odd Couple. June 27, 1973. Copyright 1973—Chicago Sun-Times. Reproduced by courtesy of Wil-Jo Associates, Inc., and Bill Mauldin.

160 Mischa Richter, "Détente." *The New Yorker*, May 6, 1974. Drawing by Richter; © 1974 The New Yorker Magazine, Inc.

16

161 Guernsey LePelley, "Do they discriminate against size?" August 22, 1969. LePelley in *The Christian Science Monitor* © 1969 TCSPS.

162 Pat Oliphant, High Lob. April 16, 1971. Editorial cartoon by Pat Oliphant. Copyright Washington Star. Reprinted with permission Los Angeles Times Syndicate.

163 Ranan Lurie. August 3, 1971. Lurie, Newsweek International. Syndicated nationally by the Los Angeles Times, internationally by The New York Times.

163 Don Wright, "Three to tango, three to tango . . ." *The Miami News*, 1971.

164 Tony Auth. *The Philadelphia Inquirer*, 1971.

164 Ray Osrin, Marco Polo. *The Plain Dealer* (Cleveland), February 17, 1972.

165 Don Wright, "I suppose you're going to tell me you were out building bridges again. . . ." *The Miami News*, 1972.

166 Pat Oliphant, "I am suddenly aware of the reason for our 20-year lack of interest." 1971. Editorial cartoon by Pat Oliphant. Copyright Washington Star. Reprinted with permission Los Angeles Times Syndicate.
167

167 Hugh Haynie, "I'm not sure of the rules, but it looks like an interesting game." *The Courier-Journal* (Louisville), July 23, 1971.

17

168 Tom Darcy. *Newsday* (Garden City, New York), 1974.

169 Gene Basset, Arms for the Love of Allah. Scripps-Howard Newspaper Alliance, January 1, 1970.

170 Bill Mauldin, "Jump off and you'll get a lifetime supply of shark repellent." March 25, 1971. Copyright 1971—Chicago Sun-Times. Reproduced by courtesy of Wil-Jo Associates, Inc., and Bill Mauldin.

171 Pat Oliphant, " 'Scuse Please—New Delivery!" May 10, 1971. Editorial cartoon by Pat Oliphant. Copyright Washington Star. Reprinted with permission Los Angeles Times Syndicate.

171 Ranan Lurie. December 1, 1971. Lurie, Newsweek International. Syndicated nationally by the Los Angeles Times, internationally by The New York Times.

172 Tony Auth. *The Philadelphia Inquirer*, 1972.

173 Don Wright, "There Goes the 8:05." *The Miami News*, 1974.

173 Tony Auth, "Peace . . ." *The Philadelphia Inquirer,* February 2, 1975.

18

174 James J. Dobbins, *Boston Herald-American,* 1973.

175 Tony Auth. *The Philadelphia Inquirer,* 1973.

176   Herbert L. Block, "Man, If You Want To Stay In This Game, You'd Better Get In Shape." February 2, 1973. Copyright 1973 by Herblock in The Washington Post.

177   John Fischetti, "Poor Fellow—First He Called Me Mr. Pompigate and Then Mr. Waterdou." *Chicago Daily News,* 1973.

177   Tony Auth. *The Philadelphia Inquirer,* February, 1974.

178   Don Wright. *The Miami News,* 1974.

178   Paul Szep, The Wonderful World of Henry Kissinger. *The Boston Globe,* February 19, 1975.

179   Bill Mauldin, "What do they mean, 'crisis in leadership'?" March 21, 1974. Copyright 1974—Chicago Sun-Times. Reproduced by courtesy of Wil-Jo Associates, Inc., and Bill Mauldin.

180   Herbert L. Block, "It's A Variation Of An Old Game—Now Hold Still." March 25, 1975. Copyright 1975 by Herblock in The Washington Post.

180   David Simpson, "Sometimes we mule skinners have to give a little ground." *Tulsa Tribune,*1975.

19

181   Neal von Hedemann. 1974. Rothco Cartoons.

182   Dennis Renault, "You're like a bunch of . . . of . . . of . . . CAPITALISTS!" *Sacramento Bee* (California), October 9, 1974.

183   Pat Oliphant, "One thing I've found out about oil . . . it's intoxicating." December 27, 1973. Editorial cartoon by Pat Oliphant. Copyright Washington Star. Reprinted with permission Los Angeles Times Syndicate.

183   Brant Parker, "Wizard of Id." March 10, 1975. By permission of John Hart and Field Enterprises, Inc.

184   Michael J. Lane. *Evening Sun* (Baltimore), 1975.

184   Ralph Dunagin, "And as a last resort in hand-to-hand combat, you can always strike the enemy with your wallet." *Sentinel-Star* (Orlando, Florida), March 12, 1975. *Dunagin's People* by Ralph Dunagin. Courtesy of Field Newspaper Syndicate.

185   Burges Green, Open Season. *The Providence Journal,* July 24, 1966.

186   Bill Mauldin, "Now that dollars are worth less, we'll need more of them." December 3, 1971. Copyright 1971—Chicago Sun-Times. Reproduced by courtesy of Wil-Jo Associates., Inc., and Bill Mauldin.

187   Al Liederman. *Long Island Press* (New York), 1974.

188   Walt Kelly, "Pogo." © 1970 Walt Kelly.

189   John Fischetti, "I Knew There'd Be a Catch in It When They Said the Meek Would Inherit the Earth." *Chicago Daily News,* 1972.

190   Joseph Parrish, Trojan Horse. 1949, Reprinted by permission of the Chicago Tribune-New York News Syndicate, Inc. All Rights Reserved.

191   Brickman, "The Small Society." *The Evening Star* (Washington, D.C.), June 7, 1966. © 1966 Washington Star Syndicate.

192   Bil Canfield, "Oh, It'll Work—Just a Matter of Getting It Started!" *Star-Ledger* (Newark), 1970.

193   John Fawcett, "—If we only had some kind of a pill." *The Providence Journal*, June 12, 1966.

194   John Hart, "B. C." 1965. By permission of John Hart and Field Enterprises, Inc.

195   Tony Auth, United Nations. *The Philadelphia Inquirer*, 1971.

196   Robert Bastian, "Of course I'm in charge—I think." *San Francisco Chronicle*, April 25, 1966. Reprinted by permission of the San Francisco Chronicle.

Index